FIRST PITCH

Winning *Money*, *Mentors*, and *More* for Your Startup

First Pitch

DEBI KLEIMAN

BABSON

FIRST PITCH

Winning Money, Mentors, and More for Your Startup

ISBN   978-1-5445-0790-3 *Hardcover*

        978-1-5445-0788-0 *Paperback*

        978-1-5445-0789-7 *Ebook*

FOR BRENT, WHO GAVE THE BEST PITCH EVER.

Contents

Introduction

As a first time entrepreneur—someone with a great business idea, a genius invention, or a brand new enterprise—you have a lot of work to do if you are going to turn your startup dream into a real-life, thriving business.

After you find or create your business opportunity, you'll need to understand your customers, learn if your product or service is feasible, figure out how to get your product or service to market, and then convince people to buy it. That's a lot. And it can be daunting.

The good news is that there is one important skill, once you get it down, that can make all the work ahead of you so much easier to accomplish.

That essential skill is, of course, pitching.

Once you learn how to create and deliver a great pitch to hold up in any situation, you will be laying the foundation you will need to succeed in almost every aspect of your entrepreneurial journey. This is why it is so important to nail pitching from the start.

Your pitch is how you explain your idea to the world. It is the primary communication tool for your startup. You need a great pitch so you can attract mentors and contacts who open the right doors to know-how and money to bring your idea to life. And eventually, you'll use your pitch to talk to potential customers, partners, and employees. It won't matter how good your idea is; if your pitch falls flat, you will be dismissed as an amateur.

Pitching is not only about presenting information on your sound business objectives; you also need to present *yourself* as an attractive future business partner. You must be able to show that you have a solid vision and the chops to bring it to fruition.

Investors and in-demand mentors see hundreds of pitches every year but only choose to work with a few. When they give their time and money to a startup entrepreneur, they do so because they feel a connection with the founder, his or her product, or more likely both. Their decisions are based on gut instinct as much as on reason. In fact, according to famed investor Howard Marks, investing decisions, including bad ones, are more likely to come from psychological factors than informational or analytical ones.

Your pitch must not only be perfect, it's got to grab 'em in the gut.

WHY DO YOU NEED THIS BOOK?

Early-stage startups, which are at the very beginning of their journey, operate with a lot of risk and unproven assumptions. This can leave you, as an early-stage startup founder, feeling at a disadvantage. The guidance I provide in this book will help mitigate that feeling by offering communication tools and strategies that will serve you not only in creating and delivering a great pitch, but in all your professional interactions as well.

I am always coming across "how-to" blogs and videos with all kinds of advice on how to give a great pitch. There is so much information that it leaves many entrepreneurs feeling overwhelmed. While much of this content can be useful, it is in disparate places and being dished out in miniature bites, which makes it extremely difficult to translate into action. If you are having trouble figuring out where to start, how to take advantage of all the advice thrown your way, and if you are struggling with what to expect in the process, you are not alone.

After talking to hundreds of early-stage entrepreneurs and conducting my own search for materials to offer my students, I became convinced that something very important was missing: a single, easy-to-follow resource that helps entrepreneurs improve their startup communication skills. This book is intended to be that resource.

To be perfectly clear, this book is not going to teach you how to be in business. You won't learn how to compile your financials or read a term sheet. It is not going to lay out the elements you need to include in your negotiations with a potential investor. And, perhaps most importantly, this book is not a magic bullet that will propel you to success if you don't have a great business idea in the first place. A great pitch will not make a bad business idea good.

This book does give you the tools and actionable steps you need to pitch your startup like a pro. It will improve your communication skills and help you speak clearly and persuasively about your new venture. And it's a one-stop resource for best practices in how to make a pitch, as well as all the vital dos and don'ts. To get you started, it provides an easy-to-implement framework that will help you create and deliver a compelling pitch to attract mentors, connections, and money.

WHY LISTEN TO ME?

Before I began teaching and working with entrepreneurs at Babson College, I earned degrees from Cornell University and Harvard Business School, which gave me a strong foundation of skills to run a business. Early in my career, I helped blue-chip consumer packaged goods companies launch new products. A decade of working at Coca-Cola, Procter & Gamble, and Welch's gave me a real-world education in classical marketing. I became an expert in brand building, product positioning, innovation, consumer insights, and how to create a winning marketing plan. My marketer's perspective has helped me solve problems and improve results in all kinds of situations throughout my career in business, so it only makes sense that I would rely on the same marketing skills and concepts to inform my approach to pitching. But more on that later.

After ten years as a brand marketer, I joined the founding team of a tech startup as head of marketing. I successfully leveraged my marketing prowess to generate buzz. We raised enough money to stage a launch, but went down in a giant ball of it-just-wasn't-meant-to-be flames. It was a great learning experience and one that gives me empathy for the trials and tribulations of other startups.

Like so many entrepreneurs before me, I dusted myself off and tried again, joining Communispace, the Boston-based consumer insight and customer-driven innovation company, during its early days. For the next five years, I ran marketing, analyst relations, and sales operations until Omnicom DAS acquired the company in a nine-figure deal.

I went from working *in* a startup to working *with* startups as president of the Massachusetts Innovation and Technology Exchange (MITX), an association of digital marketers and technologists devoted to Boston-based digital innovation. My Board of Directors and the members of MITX were among the top serial entrepreneurs and venture capitalists in Boston. It was there, after noticing a huge gap in the marketing knowledge-base of most early-stage startups, that I created, along with two co-founders, a mentoring program for entrepreneurs to connect marketing experts with Boston-based startups. Through this highly successful mentoring program, I worked with entrepreneurs in top-tier accelerator programs like MassChallenge, TechStars, and the Harvard iLab, and immersed myself in the Boston startup community.

After more than a decade of serving on startup advisory boards, coaching teams on startup marketing, and working with hundreds of brilliant entrepreneurs creating their companies, my passion for helping early-stage startups led me to my current position as executive director of the Arthur M. Blank Center for Entrepreneurship at Babson College.

The Blank Center, as the hub for startups at Babson, helps over 300 student and alumni entrepreneurs every year bring ideas to life by providing the opportunities, support, and network they need to launch businesses. I spend my days, and not a small portion of my nights and weekends, working with first-time entrepreneurs who want to learn how to pitch to investors and other key stakeholders. I've listened to over a thousand pitches, and I've seen what makes an impact and, just as importantly, what does not.

Babson has led entrepreneurship education for over twenty-five years. The heart of our mission is teaching people to become world-class leaders by thinking and acting entrepreneurially. We believe that being an entrepreneur is a *mindset*. This mindset can inform different occupations and endeavors. My approach to pitching reflects my experience as a marketer, entrepreneur, and advisor. It also draws from research and best practices at Babson.

This book is designed to give you the tools you need to understand the elements of a great pitch and how to execute one. By the time you finish this book, you will be able to incorporate into your own business orientation both the Babson bias for action[1] and a marketer's skill for communication. You will be able to create a pitch that compels investors, mentors, and others to lean in, take stock of you and your business, and give you what you need to reach the next level.

---

1   "Entrepreneurial Thought & Action," Babson, https://www.babson.edu/about/at-a-glance/entrepreneurial-thought--action/

YOUR BLUEPRINT TO THE PERFECT PITCH

This book is divided into two parts.

Part I, chapters 1 through 8, is all about the process you'll go through and the challenges you will face as you plan, write, design, practice, and deliver your pitch. At the end of each chapter you will be challenged to take action and complete an exercise. The idea is that once you go through every exercise in this part of the book, you will not only have created an individualized blueprint for your own first pitch, you will also have thought about, planned for, and developed the skills to overcome any obstacles that might cross your path.

Part II, chapters 9 through 11, covers what you need to know as you vie for visibility with angels and accelerators, seek ways to hit up family and friends, or approach other potential audiences for your pitch. There is an art to figuring out which person to approach for what purpose, and these chapters give you the insight you need to prepare for various pitch situations.

In my experience, entrepreneurs learn best from exposure to real-life examples. In the hope of providing both inspiration and instruction, I begin each chapter with a true story of how an early-stage entrepreneur used pitching skills and communication strategies to help reach their startup goals.

You can find additional information at my website thefirstpitchbook.com that will be helpful after you read the book.

Now that you have your roadmap to creating and delivering a great first pitch, turn the page and let's get started.

PART I

The Pitching Process

———

CHAPTER 1

Stories Sell

SCIENCE IN A STORY: MAKING SENSE OF MAGNOMER

Ravish Majithia invented something that can actually help save the planet.

The problem was that he had no idea how to get anyone to pay attention to his great invention or the business he was forming around it.

Ravish was a student at Babson College when we first met in 2016. He participated in Rocket Pitch, an annual Babson event where student and alumni entrepreneurs pitch their business ideas to a large roomful of students, faculty, investors, potential mentors, and startup advisors. In this fast-paced process, each person gets three minutes to tell the audience about their idea using no more than three PowerPoint slides. The goal is to get feedback on the business idea and take advantage of the opportunity to ask for help in moving their entrepreneurial venture forward. The sink-or-swim environment can be tense.

A materials engineer with a PhD, Ravish came to Babson to earn an MBA degree and to bring his idea to life. A soft-spoken man in his early thirties, Ravish used a presentation style that was understated and, for lack of a better term, nerdy. My colleagues and I had trouble following his points, and we found his presentation flat and uninspired. His Rocket Pitch was memorable, but for all the wrong reasons.

A few months later, Ravish applied for Babson's Summer Venture Program, a ten-week accelerator where participants receive intensive coaching on every aspect of their businesses, including how to create a winning pitch. Ravish had to pitch his early-stage startup as part of the Summer Venture Program application process, so I found myself watching his presentation again. This time he offered a longer, detailed version in a more intimate environment with only five of us in the room.

Even though Ravish came across as totally credible delving into enhanced plastics recycling, he struggled to explain his business or exactly what he hoped to accomplish long term He managed to convey that he was proposing some kind of venture based on a magnetic ink he had invented. Although he couldn't quite articulate it, my colleagues and I could tell he was on to something that had potential to be important.

However, his presentation was so bogged down in technical specifications of the materials and the idea that it could be applied to the recycling process—he called it *cradle-to-cradle closed-loop recycling*, industry jargon only other engineers would understand—that he failed to state directly his invention could increase the amount of plastic able to be recycled.

He neglected to emphasize the significant potential for a quadruple win: materials recovery facilities (MRFs) would make more money because they would recycle more; beverage brands and other consumer product manufacturers using the technology would earn the goodwill and competitive advantage accompanying their use of super-recyclable materials; less plastic would end up in landfills and oceans; and the company, Magnomer, had potential for profit (doing well by doing good).

Ravish was accepted into the Babson Summer Venture Program. By the end of summer, after working to identify the emotional hook and story, he knew how to give his pitch in a way that inspired listeners and made them root for the success of his enterprise. He presented his idea to an auditorium of four hundred people and crushed it. He then went on to win the MassChallenge $50,000 Gold Award after pitching in front of more than a thousand people.

Little about Ravish's actual invention changed during his time at Babson. What changed markedly, however, was his pitch and his ability to tell a story that resonated with potential investors, partners, and mentors. Ravish perfected his pitch by speaking less like an engineer and more like a storyteller. He mastered the pitch through imagery emphasizing his unique value proposition, smiling and confident the entire time.

I learned two very important things from my time as a brand marketer: stories sell, and nothing is more effective than a value proposition that connects to people's emotions.

These lessons apply equally to pitching, because much like how marketing is meant to influence people to buy something, a pitch aims to inspire listeners to provide resources to you and your startup.

Let's talk about storytelling first.

STORYTELLING IS MEMORABLE

Storytelling has been around since the beginning of time. And there's a reason for that: it's a very effective way to communicate.

By nature, people love stories. Stories are a simple way to teach people things, because all kinds of learners are able to grasp the meaning. Stories are easy to remember. Think about the last presentation you heard. How much of the data that was presented do you actually recall? How about the stories that were shared? Weren't the stories more memorable than the data?

When you pitch, you and your message should be easy to remember. Being memorable will help you develop relationships with the people you encounter. Perhaps equally important, if your story is memorable, it makes it easier for people to share with others later what they learned about you and your startup. While they may not get every detail right, the rough outlines of your story can help convey what you are working on. Your story will capture interest in you and your company.

Science supports the concept that storytelling is memorable. Organizational psychologist Peg Neuhauser found from her field studies that people learn and remember more information presented in a well-told story than when it is conveyed through facts and figures. Similarly, psychologist Jerome Bruner, in his research on storytelling, concluded that facts are twenty times more likely to be remembered when they are part of a story.[2]

Stories generally have six key components: setting, characters, plot, conflict, theme/lesson, and narrative arc. It's because of these components that stories draw people into listening mode. Stories engage the listener, and people can't help wondering, "How will this end? What will happen next?"

When people are in listening mode, they are open to new ideas, more receptive to things not heard or seen before. This contrasts to how people listen to a talk with lots of data and dry information: their brains default to evaluation mode, looking for errors in logic or judging the idea being presented. By telling a story and inviting people to stay in listening mode, you encourage them to be open to your innovation, even if they don't entirely understand it yet.

Some entrepreneurs find it difficult to tell stories, even though most people are fascinated by the backstory of why a person created a startup in the first place. I often advise entrepreneurs to use their "origin" story in their pitch. Origin stories are so personal to the entrepreneur that listeners almost always perceive

2   Boris, Vanessa, "What Makes Storytelling So Effective For Learning?" *Leading the Way* (blog). *Harvard Business Publishing,* December 20, 2017. https://www.harvardbusiness.org/what-makes-storytelling-so-effective-for-learning/

them as authentic and interesting. As a founder, only you have the ability to tell your startup story in this way; it is wholly and uniquely yours.

Another type of story people love is one that shows how your company solves a problem that makes the world, or at least a small piece of it, better. This type of story is less about looking backward into why you created the company and the problem that compelled you to start it, and more about looking forward by sharing an example of the transformation that happens because your company exists. Ravish tells this kind of story when he explains how Magnomer will revolutionize product design, using magnetic inks, to save the planet.

TIPS FOR CRAFTING YOUR STORY

When it comes to storytelling in a pitch, we can draw from the marketing world to help bring a narrative to life:

- Choose words that connect to emotion
- Employ a "show me, don't tell me" narrative
- Use metaphors or words that create an image
- Structure your story to take listeners on a "journey"

WORDS WITH EMOTION

Telling stories that use evocative words can be very effective, words that have more to them than just the plain meaning when describing the characters, conflict, and plot. Think of words that either create an image in your head or create an identifi-able feeling. For example, if you describe a product that offers a "welcoming experience," I get a feeling of warmth and family, a certain "home-y" feeling that comes with the word "welcoming." Try describing your "main character" (aka your target customer) using characteristics that have emotional, descriptive, or intangible connotations that say more than the word itself, such as "creative, outgoing, and spontaneous" or "analytical and risk-adverse."

SHOW ME, DON'T TELL ME

Another technique marketers often use is a "show me, don't tell me" narrative to create imagery in a listener's mind. For example, picture what it would be like to explore a new city while riding on a tour bus. Now think about what your impression of that same city would be if you were only looking at a map. You would have two very different experiences, and you would walk away with two very different impressions of the city.

When you're on the tour bus, a guide is *showing you* the city, engaging with you in real time. The guide points out unique aspects of the route, interesting sights you could explore during your visit. You're drawn into the story. You can't wait to see what's around the corner, what's coming next.

When you look at a map of the same city, you can easily see how to get from point A to point B. But just *telling you* what you'll see along the way does nothing to excite your senses, capture your interest, or make you want to learn more. A map tells you basic facts you need to navigate the city. A tour guide opens your eyes to why you want to visit the sights of the city. Showing landmarks, explaining history, these invite you to absorb the richness of architecture and culture.

When you're pitching, you need to take your audience on a tour of your ideas, your business, problems you encountered and how you propose to solve them. If you just hand out a "map" to prospective investors and future mentors, if you just state your problem and suggest your solution, they have nothing to relate to. They have nothing to get excited about.

USE OF IMAGERY

Using metaphors or words that have imagery associated with them can help listeners effectively grasp meaning which becomes more memorable. Sharon Sinnott, who runs Babson's Speech Center and is an expert in oral communication, likes to use this example. She asks our students, "Which works better for you: If I say let's go run a hundred yards, or if I say let's go run the length of a football field?"

Everybody knows, or at least can imagine, what running the length of a football field would be like. But it's much harder to imagine running a hundred yards. There is no image of a hundred yards to draw on, nothing to paint a picture of, and nothing to help you get a sense of what running that distance would be like. But we've all seen people run a football field. You can picture the stadium, the crowded bleachers, fans on their feet. The football player runs ten yards (first down!), then twenty yards, crosses fifty yards, all the way to the end zone (a hundred yards and touchdown!).

THE HERO'S JOURNEY, OR THE STORY ARC

Most good story arcs follow the same structure: a beginning, a middle, and an end. The scene is set at the beginning, conflict occurs as action rises in the middle, and everything comes to resolution at the end. There are more complicated versions of this, but for a story in your pitch, you don't need them. It is best to keep it simple. Think of "the hero's journey" where trials and tribulations of a hero (it should be a person, not a company) lead to a climax of a problem or crisis that ultimately finds a solution or achieves resolution. Telling a story with beginning, middle, and end (using the construct of the hero's journey) builds drama. That's where it can get really interesting.

When Ravish first pitched his original magnetic ink solution, he didn't tell his audience a story. Instead, he talked about his product idea using technical jargon and complicated concepts. And you know what? Nobody understood. And worse, nobody cared.

But when he began telling the story of his magnetic ink invention and how it could help save the planet from a horrible plastics waste problem, people got excited. They listened. When he engaged the audience by describing the problem—the Earth has a serious plastics problem and you have been duped, you have no idea how little plastic is actually being recycled—that's when he started taking investors on a journey, connecting with them through imagery. He showed mountains of plastic piled sky-high in recycling center bins, waste that would end up in landfills because there was no way to sort potential recyclables. Enter products infused with magnetic ink! See how the plastics are now sorted easily for recycling! View the mountains of plastic that have shrunk to molehills! Planet saved.

Example: Magnomer's Story Arc

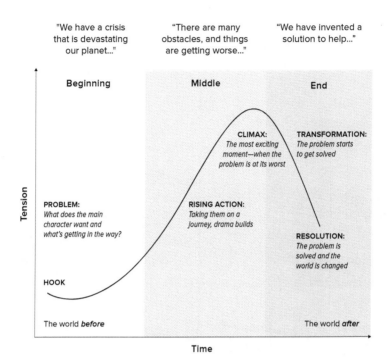

"We have a crisis that is devastating our planet..."

"There are many obstacles, and things are getting worse..."

"We have invented a solution to help..."

Tension

Time

Beginning

Middle

End

CLIMAX:
The most exciting moment—when the problem is at its worst

TRANSFORMATION:
The problem starts to get solved

PROBLEM:
What does the main character want and what's getting in the way?

RISING ACTION:
Taking them on a journey, drama builds

RESOLUTION:
The problem is solved and the world is changed

HOOK

The world *before*

The world *after*

Communication expert Nancy Duarte, in her amazing TED Talk entitled "The Secret Structure of Great Talks,"[3] offers an interesting perspective on how the hero's journey applies to presentations and speeches. She posits the idea that a presenter is not the hero of a presentation, but rather a presenter takes the audience on a hero's journey. It is the job of a presenter to escort the audience through this journey: articulating a problem, engaging the audience emotionally so they share the presenter's desire to solve the

---

3   Nancy Duarte, "The secret structure of great talks," TEDxEast, https://www.ted.com/talks/nancy_duarte_the_secret_structure_of_great_talks?language=en.

problem, then guiding them to reach the conclusion of the hero's journey, which is the presenter's solution.

Borrowing again from the marketing world, this is precisely what great marketing and advertisements do.

Take this tear-jerker of a television commercial from insurance and financial services company MassMutual. A teenage girl is sitting in front of her laptop, her parents staring over her shoulder. She clicks the laptop track pad, and then you see a close up of her face. She screams, "I got in!" The camera pans out and you see all three of them jumping and screaming.

That's it. The whole commercial consists of this one emotionally charged moment. The message? According to MassMutual, these are the moments that you, as a parent, plan for; and unless you start planning now, you're never going to be able to afford to send your kid to college.

In seconds, this ad takes something as unemotional and lackluster as saving money and heightens the tension, turning investing into a hero's journey that ends with the parents (the heroes) experiencing the relief, joy, and excitement of realizing that not only did their daughter get into college, but they can pay for it.

And it's all done through skillful imagery that connects emotionally with the audience.

CREATING A UNIQUE VALUE PROPOSITION TIED TO EMOTION

Not to get all science-y on you again, but it turns out that our brains not only like stories but our brains really like emotions, at least when it comes to making something memorable. According to developmental molecular biologist John Medina, when we experience an emotionally charged event, our brains release dopamine into our systems, making it easier for us to recall the details of the event with greater accuracy than in cases where the brain processes a blasé, everyday-type of occurrence.[4] It is likely this originated with our fight or flight instincts. In any case, this tells us that introducing emotion into pitches is an effective way to be memorable. From my time as a marketer for some of the world's best brands, I can say with total certainty that advertising which evoked emotion was far better remembered (and liked) by consumers than straightforward and boring benefit-touting advertising.

In the book *Soulful Branding,* authors Jerome Conlon, Moses Ma, and Langdon Morris discuss emotion and feelings as fundamental to how people make decisions about what they buy. "The overwhelming decisive factors in almost all human decisions are instincts, emotions, and subconsciously received signals."[5]

As an entrepreneur, you want your pitch to convince others to give you something of value—their money, their time, or their contacts. In order to get them to do this, you must trigger an

---

4   John Medina, *Brain Rules: 12 Principles for Surviving and Thriving at Work, Home, and School*, (Pear Press, 2014), 112.

5   Jerome Conlon, Moses Ma, and Langdon Morris, *Soulful Branding: Unlock the Hidden Energy in Your Company & Brand,* (CreateSpace Independent Publishing Platform; 2d edition, 2015), 13.

emotional response so they feel an affinity for your business, for you, or both.

How do you insert emotion into your pitch? The storytelling we just discussed is one way to do this.

Another part of the pitch that can be heightened with the use of emotion or emotion-laden words is your unique value proposition, your company's secret sauce, that thing it does better than anyone else. You'll use your unique value proposition, or the core of the idea, throughout your pitch and in your marketing and sales. Ideally, your value proposition will connect to your entire brand once you are up and running. It should run through the veins of the company.

While your value proposition might be related to a patented technology that creates a competitive advantage—a patent or other type of protectable intellectual property is always great to have, particularly in a very competitive space—it doesn't have to be. Your value proposition can also be the benefit a consumer derives from your product or service, something so important to the consumer that because you can do it better than anyone else, they'll choose you. Your value proposition doesn't even have to be quantifiable. Your business can offer an intangible type of value that just feels intuitively right to the consumer. It's something that meets an emotional need they may not even realize they have. The thing to remember is that it's about value, something so important that customers are willing to pay for it, not features.

Take Apple.

Apple products are not that different from competitor offerings in terms of what they actually do for people; but when the iPhone first came out, everyone was mesmerized. Apple promised and became known for a "magical" user experience; it is their unique value proposition. This user experience, embedded in how Apple products are designed, how they look, and how they work, meets an emotional need for people who want to feel delighted by their technology and viewed as a modern tech-savvy person.

Another example is BMW. Their unique value proposition of precision German engineering that creates a one-of-a-kind driving experience is summed up by their tagline: "The ultimate driving machine." If you love BMWs, you love the way your car sounds when you turn it on. You love how it feels speeding down the highway or taking a razor-sharp turn. You love how you and your "ultimate driving machine" are one. These emotions convey high value.

An entrepreneurial company example that I like is Ring. Inventor and founder Jamie Siminoff created the "smart" doorbell with video and sound streaming from your front door that you can monitor via an app on your cell phone. But these features are not Ring's unique value proposition. Rather than the tech attributes, Ring is all about neighborhood safety.

Neighborhood. Safety. Each word has a ton of meaning that resonates with consumers. "Neighborhood" makes you think of home, hearth, the streets where your kids ride their bikes. "Safety" is what we all strive for. It's what makes us comfortable and secure that our families are okay. The value of "safety" to consumers is incalculable, particularly at their homes and in their neighborhoods. Ring promises far more than just a tricked-out doorbell.

And if you need more proof that the right value proposition is worth its weight in gold, in 2018, Jamie sold Ring to Amazon for over a billion dollars, pretty good evidence that consumers thought a device promising neighborhood safety is valuable.

These examples illustrate how the right emphasis on an intangible value proposition makes a product desirable when it connects to an emotion or fills an emotional need. Apply these examples to pitching a startup. You want to convey your value proposition so it makes your startup desirable to investors and mentors. In essence, you want them to "buy" your startup.

I encourage my students at Babson to think like these companies, to consider the big picture of what their product or service means to the world, and use that as a starting point to communicate their company's unique value proposition to funders and others. You want your audience on the edge of their seats, and you will get them there by emphasizing a concept or emotion they can relate to.

WHAT'S IN A WORD? EMOTION!

Here are examples of how to transform a benefit into a word or phrase that packs an emotional punch.

Reliability = peace of mind
Convenience = freedom
Easy to use = confidence
Nutritious = feeling healthy, feeling energized
Avoid something bad = relief

In my experience, first-time early-stage entrepreneurs drill down too narrowly in the beginning. Like Ravish did at first, they get too focused on minutiae. They emphasize the "cradle-to-cradle-closed-loop-recycling" part of the story (yawn) or talk about product features rather than the big-picture value proposition. The saving-the-planet-through-recycling part of the story is going to get investors interested in learning more. As a founder, you are going to have a story that levels up to something inspiring and emotional. You just need to find it and then emphasize it when describing your business.

Go back to when you were conceptualizing your business and remember why you thought of that particular product or service in the first place. What was your reason for wanting this thing to exist in the world? Once you expose that unmet emotional need, you will find the story you are meant to tell, the one that explains the value you bring to the world.

The next step, after you've got your story and value proposition down, is to figure out how to create a pitch that flows.

TAKE ACTION: FIND YOUR UNIQUE VALUE PROPOSITION IN FOUR STEPS (A SEEMINGLY SIMPLE EXERCISE THAT IS ACTUALLY HARD TO DO)

Before diving into this exercise, you need to conduct extensive primary research with potential customers. Go out and interview (do not merely survey!) people. Ask them how they buy, what they buy, and why they buy items or services in your category today. To construct your own unique value proposition, you need this deep understanding of your customer and what they value.

Once you've completed this research, work through the following steps:

1. Make a list of what your startup does really well for your customers. Be very honest with yourself! Think of both functional (how it works) and emotional (how it makes customers feel when it works) benefits.
2. Make a list of what your closest competitors do really well. Again, don't make excuses or pretend something isn't important to the customer when you know it is.
3. From these two lists, identify one important thing you do really well that doesn't overlap with the competition. Or, identify one thing you do really well that, even though it overlaps with the competition, is significantly better than what they do or how they do it. For a unique value proposition to work, it has to be something that only you can say (hence, the word "unique"). If you say it out loud and someone could claim you are talking about another com-

pany, then you haven't done enough to identify something truly unique.

4. Now identify why this one thing is important to your customers, and express it in a short phrase or sentence that goes from the WHAT (what the thing is) to the WHY (Why is it important? How does it create value for the consumer?). Turn that benefit or feature or experience into a single word or phrase that captures the value in a way that taps into people's imaginations or emotions.

Use the format below if it helps you articulate this:

Name of company → What, Why = Word that captures value → market-facing value proposition phrase

Examples:

Boston Children's Hospital → better care, better outcomes = hope → Until Every Child Is Well™

TB12™* → training and fitness, products that help you be better and stay healthy doing what you love = longevity → Perform for Life

*This is NFL legend Tom Brady's health and fitness company.

CHAPTER 2

———

A Framework
for Flow

A MIGHTY WELL DONE PITCH

Emily Levy walks onto the stage at the Breakaway Pitch Competition with more confidence than you'd expect from a woman in her early twenties. This is a high-stakes competition, and there are four hundred people in the audience, including several well-known judges.

In a gesture of triumph, she raises her left arm and bends her elbow into a muscle pose, showcasing her patented "adaptive wear," a band of beautifully designed, breathable fabric covering the circumference of her upper arm. The band, which her company Mighty Well manufactures, hides Emily's PICC line, a long thin tube that must remain inserted into her arm so she can receive the intravenous medication she needs to treat the Chronic Neurological Lyme Disease she was diagnosed with during her sophomore year at Babson College.

Now that she has everyone's full attention, Emily launches into her pitch, explaining how she cringed when her doctor told her she must keep the tube in her arm at all times and that, if she wanted, she could cover the PICC line with a modified tube sock.

She breaks the tension recalling what she thought of the doctor's pronouncement. "Was this clueless doctor kidding? Had he ever met a college sophomore before? Did he seriously think I was going to be able to flirt with the adorable hockey player in my 8 a.m. finance class with a tube sock wrapped around my arm?"

The audience chuckles. Emily has captured their interest. Her next statement solidifies their empathy.

"I didn't want to be known as the girl with the disease."

There just had to be a better solution, Emily explains, to camouflage her PICC line in a fashion-forward way. And if *she* wanted a solution, there had to be others out there who did too.

That's how and why Emily came up with the idea for Mighty Well, a company that creates attractive and functional PICC line coverings, backpacks, and other wearable clothing and carry-gear to hide medical equipment and devices.

Emily goes on to explain that there are millions of people like herself who would jump at the chance to wear simple, comfortable, clean accessories that hide the fact that they are sick. She emphasizes how she is not her disease, how being able to appear like everyone else when out in public makes her feel like everyone else.

Everyone in the room, including me, could feel her passion and enthusiasm. Instead of self-pity, Emily exuded self-confidence about her product line and her abilities as a forward-thinking designer and entrepreneur.

Her compelling story not only won the hearts and minds of her audience, but she walked away from that pitch with $250,000 to fund Mighty Well's launch.

Telling a story with an emotional hook and having a unique value proposition that levels up beyond functional benefits, like Emily does when she pitches Mighty Well, are vital to delivering a compelling pitch. Along with appealing to audience emotions, however, you must also find a way to deliver your pitch so the audience is inclined to give you what you want. And to accomplish that, you need to create a flow for the pitch that highlights your hook while providing all the information necessary to accomplish your purpose. In this chapter, I'm going to share a framework for how to combine your story and value proposition into a full-length pitch to capture and hold audience attention. After mastering presentation flow, you will turn to chapter 3 for the specifics of how to create slides for your pitch deck.

THE IMPORTANCE OF FLOW

In a full-length pitch, one that you'd typically give to an investor or present in a formal situation, you have a very short window to convince your audience that you and your business are the real deal. Because you are usually given five to seven minutes in a pitch competition and maybe twelve to fifteen minutes in other scenarios, it's important to use your time wisely and deliver the pitch with an organized flow.

An organized flow will not only help you keep track of what you need to be saying at any given point, but also it will help the audience stay with you. Too many twists and turns or tangents can confuse the audience and cause them to disengage. While I am not recommending that you memorize your pitch or write it as script, which would sound canned and not authentic, I do advocate using a format strict enough to keep you on track, but flexible enough that it sounds natural and the audience feels engaged. I call this pitch structure the 4H Framework.

THE 4H FRAMEWORK

I developed the 4H Framework after years of observing, analyzing, constructing, and reconstructing a flow to help entrepreneurs formulate their first pitch. I came to the conclusion that all the best pitches offered the same four elements in the same order, each tying in to the venture's unique value proposition in a logical and natural way. These elements are:

- Headline: Set the context
- Heart: Make me feel something
- Head: Tell me how it works
- Hope: Inspire me with your vision

HEADLINE: SET THE CONTEXT

Your headline is your first and best opportunity to set the context of the business you are going to be talking about. It's more than a simple introduction to you, any co-founders, and your company; it's an introduction to the reason your company exists. It's a way to start setting the tone for what you are going to talk about in your pitch. The Headline should connect your product category to your value proposition in one short phrase. It needs to clearly state what your company does and its special sauce, what makes it better than any other solution to this problem. In your pitch presentation, which we cover in detail in chapter 3, your headline will be on your title slide. You don't actually read your headline. Rather, it will be up on the screen in the background, allowing your listeners a quick written introduction to your pitch while you are introducing yourself.

Because our brains are set up to crave meaning before detail, the Headline needs to convey why anyone should care about this business. Like the headline for a news article, it should provide information but also be intriguing enough to get the listener to lock-in.

There is an art to creating a short, yet memorable headline. Emily's Mighty Well pitch headline, *Wellness you can wear*, is a perfect example.

You can tell that each of these four words was carefully and artfully chosen for maximum impact. When Emily revealed her company's first slide containing only these four words, the audience instantly understood they were going to hear about something that goes on your body and is related to healthcare. The context was set, and they could start to imagine where Emily would go with her pitch. Before they had any details about this company, the audience was already leaning in, curious to learn more.

If you are pitching without a deck, as is often the case, this is the time to quickly introduce yourself and provide a quick sentence about what your pitch is going to cover that links to your value proposition, something like, *I'm excited to introduce my company Startupco. For the first time, developers can create apps in hours not days.* Then roll into the next section. When it's on the slide, you can present your headline in a format that resembles a tagline or marketing copy. But when you say it out loud without a deck, it should be more conversational, fitting into the flow of your quick introduction.

HEART: MAKE ME FEEL SOMETHING

Emily Levy had us at hello.

More accurately, I suppose, she had us the minute she lifted up her arm and showed off the Mighty Well PICC line cover. Her one simple gesture of self-empowerment, making that muscle pose, not only touched the heart of everyone in the audience, but showed how much passion she had for her product.

In her pitch, Emily said, "One in three Americans has a chronic condition. Just because you are sick doesn't mean you have to live a sick life." She was both showing and telling us in interesting and emotional terms that her product taps into a big market, that this can be a "must have" purchase for the people affected, and that the benefit of her product is more than functional, it is also emotional. Her message was that Mighty Well products can change lives.

As Emily knew, the Heart section of the pitch is where your storytelling skills make or break a presentation. The Heart section introduces a story and sets up a problem–solution dynamic. Use imagery to describe the problem you are solving, then tell a story about it and build some drama. Here you need to set up the audience to start caring about the protagonist or hero of your story. Your goal is to make the audience feel something about the problem. It can be any kind of emotional reaction, as long as it creates audience desire for the problem to be resolved.

The best way to get this level of emotional investment is to make it about an individual and their personal journey. Emily is the face of Mighty Well; her story is its story. In the Heart section of her pitch, she made everyone in the audience laugh; she inspired us, she tapped into our empathy. That's a pretty powerful combination. Anyone listening could understand why she would want this problem solved and why her solution was so compelling.

Of course not every story has that much emotion attached to it. But the more you can authentically inject drama into an experience or a problem you are describing, the more likely the audience will understand it, relate to it, and want to know more about it, including how to solve it.

Once you've described the problem in sufficient detail and laid the groundwork to reveal your solution, it's time to talk about your innovation. In the solution part of the Heart section, you should provide a very succinct description of your idea, again drawing a connection to its unique value proposition and why it's the right answer for the problem, right now. This can mean that you present data or trends to support your solution, or you talk about a gap in the market that opens the door for this opportunity; talk about why the timing is right for your solution to exist and why you are the person to bring it to life by linking back to your story.

HEAD: TELL ME HOW IT WORKS

The Head section of your pitch anticipates and answers the "how does it work" questions the audience is thinking about at this point. Compared to the Headline and Heart sections that play on emotions, the Head section is analytical and straightforward. You are describing the business model (how you make money), any underlying technology or process that creates a benefit supporting your unique value proposition, details about the market you are targeting, and how you will get people to buy.

The Head section covers market, business model, and metrics. When discussing the market, talk about how big it is, demonstrate proof for why it is growing, describe competitors and why you are better, and add a few details about target customers.

Money is all about pricing, margins, how much cash you need to keep building the company, and what you are currently spending your money on. For metrics, you'll want to showcase your assumptions around some key metrics that will drive the business, including the cost of customer acquisition, unit economics, and revenue projections, to name a few.

Each time you pitch, the Head section is going to be slightly different. Your emphasis will shift in each area depending on the specific audience. Are you pitching to an angel investor who is an industry expert, or are you in a pitch competition where a more general approach works best? How can you help them understand the mechanics of your business? As founder, you must show you have command of business details and the expert knowledge and insights to make this opportunity special for people who support your venture.

This is also the time to talk about your team. Often, early-stage investors are much more interested in the founder and their team than in business mechanics. Investors know things will change along the way. They know the target customer may change and the business model will evolve, but the people making it "go" will in all likelihood remain. Investors want to be sure the team has the experience, skills, and chemistry for the long haul, undoubtedly filled with many ups and downs.

If your team has a ton of relevant experience, connections, and domain knowledge, move it to the beginning of the Head section. This is a good opportunity to show as founder, you have that "it" factor, the ability to get people to follow you regardless of challenges ahead. Showing you can attract a top-notch team early on communicates that you are able to persuade others of your company's importance, a skill you will need to use often in your journey, a skill that investors admire.

Knit the facts and figures in the Head section into a narrative to keep hearts engaged while satisfying the business-savvy sides of listeners' brains. The consistent thread here should be your unique value proposition and how it delivers the solution people want.

In Emily's pitch, she used this time to describe her products and how she developed just the right combination of functionality and fashion. She also talked about the size of the market and showed how any companies that might be considered competitors do not create or sell items that come close to the appeal of what Mighty Well offers. Last, she talked about her current products and future additions, Mighty Well distribution channels, plans to attract and retain consumers and partners, and how to develop a community of fans. It felt very complete. She was an expert, and if asked, could easily dive into further details on any of these dimensions.

HOPE: INSPIRE ME WITH YOUR VISION

The best pitches end on a high note. According to renowned communications expert Nancy Duarte (you may recall my earlier reference to her insights on the hero's journey in chapter 1), the most compelling speeches follow a recognizable and replicable rhythm of persuasive engagement. Based at least in part on her analyses of Martin Luther King's "I Have a Dream" speech and John F. Kennedy's "We're Going to the Moon" speech, Duarte concluded that specifically going from "what is" (the world as it exists today) to "what could be" (a vision of a better world) several times in power-packed cadence creates the most engaged listeners. In designing the Hope section of your pitch, it works well to utilize this concept of moving from "what is" to "what could be."

While nobody expects an early-stage entrepreneur's pitch to move mountains, you can paint an inspiring picture of what the world would be like when your startup achieves huge success.

Like other aspects of your pitch, this vision or Hope narrative should be conveyed in a story-like way, using emotional words and imagery to show the impact your idea can have to make the world better, at least in some small way. Here the unique value proposition is the fuel to power this vision. Be sure to remind the audience of this.

End your pitch with a vision of hope, and you will inspire your listeners to want to be a part of your creation. This is the goal, to get them to lean in and want to be involved.

By the time Emily reached the Hope section of her Mighty Well pitch, you could almost feel the audience excitement. She wanted to help "patients and their caregivers turn sickness into strength." She wanted to lead a global charge to change perceptions of patients, making them "fighters not victims." What started as a stylish piece of fabric to cover a PICC line transformed into a global movement to change how people think. Pretty good vision of hope, I'd say.

TAKE AIRBNB, FOR EXAMPLE

When I teach how to pitch to entrepreneurs at Babson, I like to cite a company and brand familiar to all, Airbnb, and discuss how I would have pitched the company using the 4H Framework in 2009 when it was just a startup.

Back in 2009, Airbnb's value proposition was fairly revolutionary, the idea that a budget traveler who wanted to experience a new place like a local and embrace the vibe of a new city could find accommodation in someone's private home.

AIRBNB'S HEADLINE

The first slide would contain the line "Book Rooms with Locals, Rather than Hotels."[6]

With just seven words, this headline reveals the company's category and main functionality, and connects to its value proposition. In true 4H form, this headline does much with little. I would introduce myself while the audience is looking at this slide and settling in.

AIRBNB'S HEART

In the Heart section, I would tell the true story of my recent trip to Spain, which clearly highlights the problem Airbnb was created to solve, as well as revealing functional and emotional reasons why travel without Airbnb is a losing proposition.

I would detail how my trip to Barcelona failed to meet every expectation of an exciting and memorable trip. My narrative would sound something like this:

> I was traveling on a budget, but because my trip was during high season, I ended up having to book a hotel that cost more than I wanted to spend. While it was painful to use up so much of my funds on accommodations—money I would have preferred to spend on travel experiences that would have given me the culture and adventure I was hoping for—I had no other viable options. To make matters worse, the hotel was in a tourist district, and I was oblivi-

---

6   This was the text on the first slide actually used by Airbnb in its pitch deck. Although the founders of Airbnb didn't have the 4H Framework when they created their deck, it's interesting to see that their narrative did, indeed, follow its flow. If you'd like to check it out for yourself, Airbnb's original pitch deck is online at https://www.slideshare.net/PitchDeckCoach/airbnb-first-pitch-deck-editable.

ous to the fact that the side of Barcelona I was seeing was about as authentic as Disneyland. I didn't know until later that I had missed all the amazing parts of the city that tourists don't typically see. Because I stayed in a hotel so far away from where locals hang out, I missed the opportunity to immerse myself in the culture and pulse of a city I had dreamed of visiting all my life.

I'd go on to explain that I would have loved to have had a real Barcelona connection, someone to show me around, tell me where to find the best tapas and which shops had the best quality (and reasonably priced) ceramic cookware. I wish I had an insider's advice on off-the-beaten-track art galleries or where to see an authentic flamenco show. Experiencing Barcelona like a local would have made the city come alive for me.

I'd embellish the story further, building up the drama around how touristy it was where I stayed. I'd throw in an anecdote of how I misunderstood something about Barcelona because I didn't get to experience it like a local. I'd want to show the problem, an expensive and unspectacular visit to Barcelona, and reveal the solution that would have, should have, could have been Airbnb.

I would also have wanted to be clear about who I had created Airbnb for, the budget traveler, and how with this target customer in mind, I would create a buying experience to meet their needs.

AIRBNB'S HEAD

For the Head section, I would talk about how the budget travel market is huge, and how easy it is for anyone in this market with a simple internet connection to search cities and listings and book right on the Airbnb platform. I would take great pains to distinguish my cutting-edge company from Craigslist, where user experience is, to put it mildly, suboptimal. Unlike Airbnb, if hosts who have a room to rent to travelers don't post every day on Craigslist, their post goes down to the bottom of the list. I would explain that when these same hosts post on Airbnb, they only have to post their listing one time. After they create a single detailed profile that is easy to read and review, they can sit back and watch the bookings roll in.

I'd emphasize that in Airbnb's two-sided market, everybody wins: the traveler can stay with a local at a place that's highly reviewed, the host earns money on their empty room, and both get to meet someone from another city or country. Talking about the competitive set, it would be easy for anyone watching my pitch to see why Airbnb offers an opportunity to do something truly different and better.

I would explain all this using words and imagery that convey the simple user experience, painting a clear picture of how the company works and why it is both beneficial and desirable for travelers to have the freedom to book online travel and stay with a local. And I'd explain that hosts would jump at the opportunity to pursue the financial freedom that comes with gaining additional income on an asset they already have but don't use. I would add that this business model is scalable and has inherent network effects that allow it to grow simply by running it.

For this section, I would note that we take a percentage of every booking, and I would tackle questions around the risky elements of this product. For example, how do we ensure traveler safety and build trust. I know these questions are on listeners' minds. I would try to remove objections as quickly as they occur.

AIRBNB'S HOPE

Finally, I'd bring it home in the Hope section, the goal being to get my audience to want to be a part of changing the world of travel.

I'd begin with my vision, inviting them to picture a world where people connect like never before, where travel expands into a new dimension, and where unused space takes on a new meaning. I would describe how travelers immerse themselves in new places with a local to guide them, and hosts are able to transform unused living quarters into welcoming (and profitable) lodgings.

Then I would invite the audience to be an integral part of transforming travel as we know it, to make a difference by helping the world become a more connected place.

If you were in those investors' shoes, wouldn't you have jumped on the chance to help turn this amazing vision into an equally amazing new company?

I'd say the 4H Framework holds up pretty well for Airbnb. You might try this exercise yourself. Think of a company that is extremely successful today and imagine it as an early-stage startup. How would you as founder have pitched the company?

While I've explained the 4H Framework in the context of a full-length pitch, it works equally well for the flow of shorter pitches.

Each section is covered with the same overall goal, just in less time with less information.

With your new skills in storytelling and creating emotional hooks, along with the 4H Framework flow, you now have the tools to create a presentation deck for a full investor pitch. Chapter 3 will describe best practices for creating professional slide deck content. Later in chapter 5, we will cover deck design principles.

TAKE ACTION: CREATE YOUR 4H FRAMEWORK FLOW

Craft a bulleted list for each section of the pitch: Headline, Heart, Head, and Hope. Remember to check that your unique value proposition is present in some way for each section.

Headline
Write a few takes on a headline, use only five to nine words. It can be either a phrase or a full sentence. It doesn't matter as long as you center it on your "special sauce" or unique value proposition. Ask yourself whether each word is working hard to convey meaning.

Heart
As you develop an outline of your story to tell for the Heart section, write some bullets about the problem and the solution. Add at least two bullet points on who the target customer is. Use descriptive words, not demographics.

Be sure to create drama, infusing emotions into the problem-solution scenario. Try playing with different emotions that connect to your value proposition. Keep doing this until one feels right.

Reorder these bullets until it feels like you have a story flow with a beginning, a middle, and an end.

Head

Your list of bullet points for the Head section should include anything that would help someone understand how your business works. You'll also need a bullet on market opportunity (size, growth), the team, and a specific but simple statement about how you make money.

Hope

As you conjure your Hope section, imagine a scenario where the big vision of where you want to take this idea long-term can change the way the world looks or works for your target customer. This should feel inspiring but not inauthentic. Write, in two to three bullets, words or phrases that capture inspiring elements of this new world. Can you capture what this looks and feels like?

Putting It All Together

Once you feel comfortable with your bullets for each section, practice saying them out loud until you find the right flow. Don't write a script and don't memorize. Just use the concepts you have bulleted out in the Headline, Heart, Head, and Hope order to make it flow. If it doesn't feel natural in terms of the flow, try to reorder the bullets within a section until it does.

CHAPTER 3

Create the Perfect Pitch Deck

PITCH DECK POLISH: TAYLOR CUSTOM RINGS

Jerry Taylor knows diamonds and gemstones. As a certified graduate gemologist who trained at the prestigious GIA in California, he also knows that lab-grown diamonds and mined diamonds are identical when it comes to their physical, optical, and chemical properties.

According to Jerry, however, what makes lab-grown diamonds stand out is that, unlike their mined counterparts, they are environmentally friendly and free from political conflict, and they do not rely on child labor to produce. Adding to the positive attributes of lab-grown diamonds, they are about 20 percent less expensive than mined diamonds, which has spurred a rise in consumer interest. In fact, research reveals that many consumers, particularly socially conscious ones who make up a large part of the generation currently buying engagement rings, prefer lab-grown diamonds, citing environmental damage caused by diamond mining as reason enough to move to manufactured stones.

Jerry knew there were huge possibilities to create a business around lab-grown diamonds; and his wife Ashley, then an MBA student at Babson, agreed. Together the couple decided to go all-in on their e-commerce startup, Taylor Custom Rings.

The idea for Taylor Custom Rings was to create custom-designed rings out of lab-grown diamonds and recycled metals, incorporating other materials and approaches to appeal to the socially conscious consumer whenever possible. While Jerry leveraged his diamond expertise in the business, Ashley, inspired by her late grandmother's appreciation for natural beauty and quality materials, became the creative force behind the ring designs. Together, their goal was to create an experience around a moment, while reducing what is typically a huge expense for most people, buying an engagement ring.

The couple-turned-business-partners had all the elements needed to create a great pitch: a solid value proposition from which to draw a meaningful headline, a compelling solution to both a global and a common personal problem, a large target market supported by solid metrics that lent credence to the viability of their enterprise (the "Head" portion of a pitch), and a vision of hope that both the environment and the pocket-books of couples starting out on their marriage journey would benefit from Taylor Custom Rings. What's more, they knew how to leverage these elements to create a captivating pitch deck, one supporting a pitch that won the couple more than $30,000 at the B.E.T.A. Challenge new venture competition.

Your pitch deck, that small but potent group of presentation slides, is the most powerful visual tool you have to communicate about your startup in its early days. As the Taylor's story demonstrates, if you can package all the amazing details about your business in a compelling visual way, you will significantly increase the impact of your pitch.

Not only must your pitch deck perfectly complement your verbal pitch or "talk track," but in one form or another, it can act as your business plan now and in the future. In fact, pitch decks are a requirement for almost every communication and presentation you will make about your company. Plan on using some version of a pitch deck for everything from attracting investors and mentors to introducing your company to potential employees, bankers, advisors, early adopters, and others.

Your pitch deck is the most important tool in your early startup arsenal, and it is going to have to do a lot of work: communicate the ins and outs of your business, represent who you are, and relay exactly why this business absolutely must exist. Not only should your pitch deck content convey all this information, it has to do so without a lot of words while looking polished and well-produced. Remember, the purpose of a pitch deck is not to replace your talk track, but to support it.

As you create your own great pitch deck, there are a few general rules that I recommend you keep in mind:

- Reveal your idea or solution upfront (don't keep your audience waiting).
- While you should pay attention to best practices, never sac-

rifice your authenticity, the flow that works for you, in favor of a pre-set outline.

- Present each slide as simply as possible. Remember that your accompanying talk track will explain the points your slides emphasize.
- Try to keep your presentation at fifteen to eighteen slides total, including the title slide and any additional slides in your appendix. In fact, the shorter the deck the better.
- Try to keep your presentation to under fifteen minutes.

Let's first look at best practices for slide deck content. Later in chapter 5, we'll talk about best practices for design.

PITCH DECK CONTENT BEST PRACTICES

In the last chapter we talked about how to design a great pitch flow using the 4H Framework. Now, I am going to address how to create an ideal deck to support that flow using what I consider best practices for a pitch deck.

In general, there are eleven "must have" slide segments for a full-length investor pitch deck, with additional slides that can be added in an appendix when necessary.[7]

Please note that I refer to these as slide segments for a reason. While one slide should suffice for most segments, in some instances you might need two or more slides to make all your points.

---

7   Note that I'm expressing this list as if you are using PowerPoint or Keynote or Google Slides. If these` kinds of programs don't appeal to you, there are other ways to visually present such as Prezi or pre-designed templates you can find on the internet.

When following the 4H Framework storytelling flow, your pitch slides will appear as:

Headline: Set the context

Slide 1: Title slide

Heart: Make me feel something

Slide 2: Problem

Slide 3: Solution

Head: Tell me how it works

Slide 4: How it works

Slide 5: Market opportunity

Slide 6: Competition

Slide 7: Team

Slide 8: Basic financials or metrics

Slide 9: Go-To-Market

Slide 10: The ask

Hope: Inspire me with your vision

Slide 11: Big close

Appendix

Let's walk through each slide segment in the context of the 4H arc to understand exactly what information it should contain.

HEADLINE: SET THE CONTEXT

Slide 1: Title

Your title slide reveals your headline, that concise statement or phrase to provide important context for what your company and presentation will be about. This sets up your audience with the right mindset and forms a starting point for them to take in your message. Remember, the brain craves meaning before detail.

For Taylor Custom Rings, I've seen Ashley use *Dramatically Change the Impact of Your Jewelry*, an extremely powerful title slide statement. Every word contributes to supporting the value proposition that your jewelry impacts you and the planet, and it's also custom-designed just for you, making a fashion impact.

This simple Headline slide makes you curious to learn exactly how you can change the impact of your jewelry purchase. It gets you to sit up and listen. That's a powerful punch packed into seven words.

I've also seen Ashley use the line, *Yours. Not mined.* on her title slide. This is also quite effective, and can do double-time as a marketing tagline. Because their brand says what they do, custom rings, they can use a shorter headline like this. It provocatively sets the stage for what's coming next.

TAYLOR
CUSTOM RINGS
Yours. Not mined.

It's important that your Headline slide incorporate your logo. I'll explain more about the importance of a well-crafted logo later when we explore pitch deck design.

HEART: MAKE ME FEEL SOMETHING

Slide 2: Problem

As you will recall, the Heart section is where you can tell a story about your reason for being or how you will transform the world by solving a problem. You're telling a story about a hero who needs to right a wrong in the world. You use Slide 2 to sum up the problem you're trying to solve, while Slide 3 will offer your solution.

It's important for Slide 2 to grab people's attention. If you lose them here, you are done for the day. There are various techniques presenters can use in this regard.

You could provide a provocative claim or piece of data about how the world works today related to your problem. For example, the Taylors might use something like this:

> Did you know that diamond mining causes soil erosion, deforestation, and ecosystem destruction?

Another effective tactic is to ask the audience to raise their hands (self-identify) if they can relate to the problem being addressed. For example, in their presentation for Taylor Custom Rings, the Taylors might present a slide that asks:

> How many people here have ever bought or received a diamond ring?

> How many of you know exactly where that diamond came from?

Chances are the majority of the audience is going to answer the first question in the affirmative and the second in the negative. After eliciting a response, the presenter can move into an explanation of parts of the world where mining is exceptionally horrible, causing massive environmental and social damage, and how she learned about it.

In other instances, I've seen presenters challenge the audience to picture a certain scenario, asking them to imagine a scene where a particular problem is occurring. Sometimes, merely challenging the audience to consider how they would feel if a certain thing happened to them or to those they care about serves as a shortcut to dramatically highlighting the problem.

When presenting the problem that Taylor Custom Rings is going to solve, Ashley shows an image of a diamond mining site that covers the entire slide. It's a grim-looking scene, a giant hole in the ground with gritty, dirty buildings surrounded for miles by a desolate landscape. Overlaid on this slide is the text:

> Diamond mining has caused immense human suffering and environmental degradation.

When Ashley displays this slide, her talk track covers environmental devastation and humanitarian crises that result from diamond mining. She's telling a story. The photograph is so completely opposite to the beauty one thinks of in a diamond that it's shocking, and the audience is instantly hooked.

Slide 3: Solution

Where Slide 2 begins the introduction to the company story, Slide 3 explains how the company will give the story a happy ending, relieve the pain, fill the need, or solve the problem.

It is here you answer provocative questions of "what if" and "imagine yourself" which the audience considered in the problem slide. The goal here is to provide a resolution to their distress. This is where you start hammering home your company's unique value proposition, what makes it so special.

In the Taylors' pitch deck, the solution slide segment is presented as a very short video showing how a lab-grown diamond is made. The video runs silently in the background as Jerry talks about how lab-grown is truly identical to a mined diamond. After showing what a clean, scientific, and modern process manufacturing diamonds is, Jerry drives the solution home by presenting a slide to show both diamond types are chemically, physically, and optically identical.

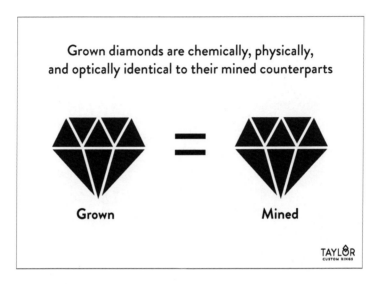

His next slide sets the stage for the ensuing Head section, consumer trend data showing that the modern consumer (aka the millennial) prefers lab-grown diamonds, and that this preference is increasing.

Modern Consumers Prefer Grown Diamonds

Over the past three years, 95% of our customers
have chosen lab-grown over mined diamonds.
Recent research shows similar trends:

66%

of millennial consumers
will consider grown diamonds.
(Up 13% from 2017)

23%

of millennial consumers
will definitely buy a
lab-grown diamond.

TAYLOR
CUSTOM RINGS

They've now established a big market with an upward trend supported by numbers.

Remember, the format and order of slides are meant to help you create high-impact flow for your presentation. I always recommend that if you do have some noteworthy business traction you can highlight, such as a decent monthly recurring revenue, some great beta clients, or impressive revenue growth, that you add a slide on this and place it immediately after the problem and solution slides. Demonstrating traction with key numbers showing people like what you have can generate excitement. Where it makes sense, don't hesitate to go a bit off linear track to create the best presentation that is authentic to you and your pitch.

HEAD: TELL ME HOW IT WORKS

The Head section will be the longest of your deck. It presents the unique challenges of showcasing your business acumen and your enterprise viability without overwhelming your audience with minutiae or complex explanations.

Generally, when presenting business elements in the Head section, make your points on the slide using as few words as possible. Numbers are great support points. I've seen people use a single slide with a single number displayed in giant text, for example $10 billion, to explain market size. This drives home that it's big while relying on the talk track to explain the number and its significance. Using stand-alone icons or symbols on pitch slides is also an effective way to dramatically support your points.

Slide 4: How it works

For the Slide 4 segment, you will be showing how your product or service works at a very high level, while your talk track fills in the details.

For a food or beverage company, this could mean bulleting out where ingredients were sourced from or using data on trends that support your talk track explanation of why your offering is relevant and timely.

For a tech product, you might use a process diagram, noting main steps or screenshots from the platform, of how a customer would experience using the product. This should be conveyed very simply, using only one or two slides that give an overview of the process.

To demonstrate how their online custom ring-making design

and ordering system works, the Taylors show screenshots of the website pages customers visit during the process of customizing a ring. These pages display the shapes, metals, and sizes offered. This is an effective way to show not only how elegantly the system works, but also product design options and prices for every budget. The slides reinforce their talk track covering how easy and beautiful the whole Taylor Custom Ring design and ordering experience is.

SHOULD YOU DEMONSTRATE A PRODUCT IN THE MIDDLE OF A PITCH?

Demo-ing a product in the middle of a pitch is generally a bad idea.

If you are presenting a tech product, think about all the things that could go wrong in a live demo. You could lose your internet connection or you might experience some kind of unanticipated glitch, especially if you are still building out your platform. Your goal is to get to the next meeting. Save your live demo for that up-close-and-personal meeting with the investor. Instead, use screenshots or, to get even more sophisticated, record a video (created with software like Brainshark) of a key process on the platform that runs in the background (on the slide) while you talk about it at a high level.

If you are pitching a food product, you want your audience focused on you and your pitch, not on inhaling the world's greatest quadruple chocolate confection that you created to corner the snack market. In this case, by all means serve up samples of your delicious sweets to the audience, but not until the end of your presentation.

You want all eyes and ears focused on you and your deck. The fewer distractions, the better.

Slide 5: Market opportunity

Next up is the market opportunity slide segment.

In the startup world, timing is everything, and the purpose of this slide segment is to help explain why now is the right time for your idea or business to take off. Since you are likely going to talk about trends here, it's a good idea to show some support data to bolster credibility. (Be sure to provide citations to your sources.)

It is important that the slide supporting your position not only demonstrates growth in your market, but also that you are at the beginning of a big sea change in the industry. Sometimes, this might be a forward-looking statement that reflects a theory you have about how the market will evolve over the next several years. In this case, the data you show could highlight an inflection point, or how different and seemingly unrelated trends are converging. This is a perfect way to show how the opportunity you have identified is special and that you have insight on how it will grow. Use graphs and charts from your research that are easy to read and that emphasize your points.

The Taylors accomplish this by presenting a slide that looks ahead at projected growth of the lab-grown diamond market in the current year, and then five and twelve years out.

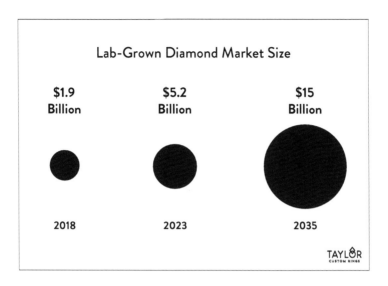

In this segment, you also want to demonstrate that you have undertaken a complete analysis of the customer. This isn't merely generic demographics. Ideally, you will provide a visual demonstration to reflect your deep understanding of your customer: their beliefs, values, and buying behavior, including how your solution addresses their problem.

You can use photographs, data, or icons to support the points you make about your target customer. You also want to quantify the target market population you think you can realistically reach and then expect to win. Typically, these metrics are shown in the form of a slide containing a pie chart or diagram of concentric circles with values in each. Think of a bullseye target with each concentric circle winnowing down as you identify your target market. The graphic will reflect the TAM (total addressable market), the SAM (serviceable available market, or the segment your product can reach), or the SOM (serviceable obtainable market). The SOM is your goal.

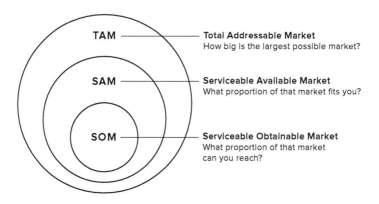

TAM SAM SOM Explained

TAM — Total Addressable Market
How big is the largest possible market?

SAM — Serviceable Available Market
What proportion of that market fits you?

SOM — Serviceable Obtainable Market
What proportion of that market can you reach?

Slide 6: Competition

Next, you want a slide that portrays the competition. This is where you can demonstrate your expert knowledge and show that you understand the industry and what your competitors are currently doing.

It's not enough to just list competitors. You should be able to provide some perspective on what they are good at and not so good at.

The way to demonstrate this visually on a slide is to plot the competitors on a "map" of the industry. Sometimes this is called a *two-by-two* where you would choose two key dimensions that people look for when buying in your market and plot the competition according to how they deliver on those dimensions.

To plus up your analysis of the competition, think about showing the magnitude of the threat, building your credibility as you showcase your knowledge of industry dynamics. How likely is the competition to create something similar to what you offer?

To show magnitude, you could make each competitor's dot reflect the size of the threat: the bigger the dot on the map, the bigger the competitive threat. If there are many competitors in the space, select only a couple to mention in order to make the point without belaboring it.

Example of a Competitors 2x2

See more examples at TheFirstPitchBook.com

Another way I've seen entrepreneurs tackle the competition is to create a key benefits comparison, sometimes called a *power grid*. This lists the main benefits of your product in this space in priority order, as determined by the target customers, listed down vertically. Across the top of the grid is your company and then three to four competitors. The grid is completed with checkmarks showing which companies deliver on the key benefits listed. Your startup should check most, if not all, of the boxes.

A CHART IS WORTH A THOUSAND WORDS

Anywhere in a pitch that you can provide quantifiable data in chart form is going to be helpful. Images and graphics are shortcuts to help people easily understand this type of information. There are many ways to graph data, so make sure what you are showing is both relevant to the argument you are making and also easy to decipher.

In some cases, that might mean reducing your data to a pie chart or a bar chart. Be sure that any labeling on your chart is in a font large enough that it can be read from the back of the room. Investors see hundreds of pitch decks a year, so make it easy for them to get what's special about you and your business.

Slide 7: Team

The team slide is next and is very important. As I've mentioned previously, with early-stage companies, investors know there could be multiple pivots and changes to your business model and even to the target customer. However, the team should be a constant (hopefully). The team slide should show why your team is uniquely qualified to establish and grow your business by showcasing its credibility based on the team's education, past experiences, or industry connections.

You don't need to provide much information on each team member. Just include a photo, what their role is, and two or three lines about what makes each of them valuable to the venture.

In the Taylor Custom Rings pitch, it's extremely relevant that Jerry is not only a Certified Graduate Gemologist but also that he has access to the world's best lab-grown diamonds. Ashley, who holds an MBA, has creative experience that makes her designs unique. These things are special about this founding team and inspire confidence in their ability to execute the idea.

If you're an early-stage entrepreneur and don't have a lot of experience, you won't have much to tout. Use what you have to the best effect, like logos of where you went to school, jobs you've previously held, or a phrase about a project or internship you worked on that required skills similar to those you'll use for your startup. You might also consider including information about your advisors or other investors who have agreed to work with you if you are light on team credibility.

Slide 8: Basic financials or key metrics

Often investors will be looking for some elements of the financial picture of the startup. You are not required to provide a full Profit and Loss (P&L) statement or balance sheet. This kind of financial detail can be hard on the eyes in a slide presentation.

It's not that you shouldn't build financial models to support how your idea will grow into a scalable business; you definitely need to do this, probably forecasted out eighteen months to two years with logical assumptions you can explain. While much of your financial modeling will be based on speculation, how you explain your assumptions will tell an investor about you as a founder. However, this detailed financial model doesn't go into the pitch deck. This would be something you'd go over with an investor when you get to the next meeting. However, if you want to have some topline financials ready in case you get a question best answered with financial detail, you could have a slide in the appendix.

For purposes of your pitch deck, create a slide or two supporting the key metrics you are tracking, or some basic financial indicators, such as percent margin or unit economics. If you have enough data to show a trend, for instance something that indicates consistent revenue growth month over month, this is good information to highlight in the deck using a graph.

Slide 9: Go-To-Market

The go-to-market segment is where you would show the sales and marketing plans you have created to launch the product or grow your reach, how you will attract target customers, and how you will retain those customers.

Other information you might include on a go-to-market slide

includes either your sales channels or distribution partners (using their logos to represent them), your pricing strategy (shown as tiers or packages), or how you will market in both paid and organic ways. You should also consider listing logos of the media channels (online and offline) you will be leveraging to reach your target audience, such as LinkedIn ads, a particular industry newsletter, Instagram influencers, or Bloomberg News online, among others. And if you have unique tactics and strategies for driving customer adoption, by all means present that in a slide to emphasize your innovative marketing plans.

Other key performance indicators (KPIs) or metrics you can show in this segment include the return on investment (ROI) from beta customers, as well as your actual or anticipated customer acquisition costs (CAC) and how they are calculated.[8]

The Taylors, in their pitch deck, summarize results in a couple of different slides (rings sold to date, consumer social media engagement) and future goals on various social channels where they sell and engage influencers, as well as conversion rates from paid search, website improvements, and email marketing campaigns. An example of one is shown.

---

8   The CAC is the sum of all the things you did (or plan to do) to market and sell, including things like paid advertising, trade shows, salespeople, even interns, over a period of time, divided by the number of new customers you get (or hope to get) from these activities over the same period of time. Quarterly is a good time frame to use. This number should go down over time. You should be able to describe how it will decrease as you scale up.

We've Set the Stage to Launch Our Website

Built Key
Website Tool

Designed New
Line of Rings

Created Key
Partnerships

800

Rings Sold

25,000

Followers on Instagram

TAYLOR
CUSTOM RINGS

Slide 10: The ask

You begin to wrap up your pitch when you move to the use-of-funds slides or "the ask."

If it's an investor meeting, you will state how much you want to raise and include some detail about how you will use the money. Here you would probably want to present a clean, well-organized chart with one column listing things you want the money for and another column indicating a correlating milestone. For example, if you have a goal to raise $300,000, you would show in a clear manner how you will use that money:

1. $50,000 toward paid digital advertising on Facebook and Instagram to drive customer adoption
2. $100,000 to hire a salesperson
3. $150,000 for technical development/product improvements

It's a good idea to show any goals you have set for each of these, being explicit about where you expect to be in a certain amount of time for each milestone as a result of the spend. For example, that $100K salesperson should get you to $1 million ARR (annual run rate) in twelve months.

Remember that an investor will be trying to find ways to de-risk the investment as they are viewing your pitch. In the use-of-funds slides, you want to show how this money will allow you to confirm assumptions you are making about how it will work. This will take some risk out of the startup because you will have proven or disproven something crucial to the business model.

Generally, I would not advise that you present any information in your deck about valuation. That is a topic to address much later in the process. The goal of this meeting and early startup pitch deck is to get to the next meeting.

HOPE: INSPIRE ME WITH YOUR VISION
Slide 11: Big close

As we showed in the last chapter, it's very effective to wrap up the pitch with the Hope section, sharing your vision about how the world will be changed because your innovation exists. Here, you will want to re-invoke the emotional story you told at the beginning, using words or images that inspire your audience with your bold picture of success.

The Taylors' pitch for Taylor Custom Rings ends with their mission to "help the world fall in love with grown diamonds" and comes with an invitation to join them. The imagery behind the words covers the entire slide, a couple embracing, in beautiful natural outdoor surroundings. The picture in subtle undertones repeats their main messages and value proposition, tightly told.

Now, a bonus pro tip: if you are presenting to a large group, like a demo day or pitch competition, be sure to display your contact information (email and/or cell phone number) on the very last slide so that people can get in touch with you if they would like to offer feedback, a connection, or help.

APPENDIX

Many pitch decks include an appendix. The appendix can hold multiple items in it and is a handy place for slides that will support your answers to some of the more obvious questions you know you will be asked, such as:

- The customer acquisition cost (CAC) calculation
- Additional trend data to support industry knowledge or market dynamics knowledge
- More data about the customer's behavior or attitudes
- A short case study
- Further competitive analysis
- The advisory board that is helping you, if you didn't show it earlier
- Some financials like cash flow so you can talk about monthly burn rate
- Data to justify your pricing strategy

Now that you have an idea how highlights of your pitch will unfold in an actual pitch deck for a full-length presentation, you can use these slide categories and segments in other types of pitches. At the end of this chapter, you'll find a Take Action exercise to help you get started on creating your own full-length pitch deck.

VARIATIONS ON A THEME

Think of the full-length pitch deck we just covered as your main version. As you continue on your entrepreneurial journey, you will come across scenarios where you will want to create variations of the original deck.

One variation to keep in your arsenal is what is referred to as a mail-ahead deck, a shorter version designed to generate interest in setting up a meeting with you. Typically, the mail-ahead deck will be attached to an email introduction. It should be no more than ten slides, just enough to whet a person's appetite. In fact, the shorter your mail-ahead deck, the better; you don't want to give away too much before you give your actual full-length pitch.

You will also want to create a leave-behind deck containing more information than the full-length, live, pitch deck you actually present. The purpose of the leave-behind deck is to provide an easy resource for members of your live audience to explain your presentation to others in their firm or network who did not attend your pitch. Think of it as a tool for interested audience members to use in advocating for your company to their peers.

The leave-behind deck will generally contain the same slides as your pitch deck, but individual slides will offer more text in order to fill in the details you covered in your talk track. Don't go overboard with the text, though. Each slide still needs to be readable, interesting, and clean enough to not overwhelm.

You can find examples of all kinds of pitch decks by searching online or visiting my website thefirstpitchbook.com. Get inspired by how some of the best companies have represented their stories. Read them to find approaches you might like to use in your own deck.

PITCH DEVELOPMENT CATALYZES IMPORTANT THINKING

One of the great advantages of digging into the full-length pitch flow and creating a pitch deck is the opportunity it gives you to delve into the details of your business, pinpoint weak areas, and use that knowledge to improve your business model.

Practically every entrepreneur I have worked with, from first-time early startup founders to seasoned serial entrepreneurs, tells me how much they learn about their business through the process of developing a full-length pitch. Pitch development helps expose any wrong assumptions or holes in logic. Missing information is identified. The business as a whole will become stronger for having gone through the rigors of the pitch development process.

Another benefit of creating a full-length pitch is that it forms the basis for developing other types of pitches, especially its shorter cousins, the elevator pitch and the rocket pitch. Believe it or not, these can be difficult to create if you haven't already gone through the full-length process.

In the next chapter, I'll show you how to draw on pitch-creating skills you've now acquired to create other pitch forms that pack a powerful punch.

LET YOUR PITCH DECK MULTITASK

Your pitch deck is more than a tool to attract investors. It's a resource to communicate the story of your business in a variety of contexts to different audiences. In creating your deck, you distilled key elements of your company down to a clear, compelling story. A natural extension is to take this communication tool that reflects the best of who you are and redesign it to project your message to other audiences.

Pitch Deck as Business Plan

The purpose of presenting a business plan to another person, whether it's a member of your executive team, a partner, or your banker, is to form a connection to get their buy-in for your venture. Your pitch deck can serve this purpose well. It is chock full of vital information written to be compelling and persuasive. People have short attention spans; they don't generally want to wade through a lot of information. A fifteen-slide, leave-behind, pitch-deck-turned-business-plan covers all your business basics while still packing an emotional punch.

Pitch Deck for Recruiting and Onboarding

Modified slightly for recruitment and onboarding, your pitch deck can serve as a powerful introduction to your company for prospective and new employees. It communicates the passion, purpose, and values of your company.

Pitch Deck as Marketing Tool

As your company grows, you may find yourself reaching out for marketing and corporate communications support. Working with outside creatives is a highly personalized experience, and finding the right fit depends as much on compatibility as it does on talent. Presenting your pitch to marketing partner candidates will not only help them understand your vision and mission, but also it will help you observe their reaction to assess whether they could be a good fit for your organization as you grow your brand. Your pitch will serve as an invaluable guide, setting the tone for creatives who develop your marketing messages and materials.

Pitch Deck to Inform (Not Replace!) Your Sales Pitch

An investment pitch is not and never should be a sales pitch. While it can and should be informed by your pitch deck, your sales deck will have elements that are more product-focused and customer-focused. It will not include things like financials or a go-to-market plan, but it should include information that helps with credibility and reputation, such as the team members behind the company and metrics that support any traction your product is getting, maybe showcasing logos of companies you are working with.

Be sure to include messaging that creates the most solid emotional connection with your audience. In the same way you research your potential investors in order to find commonalities on which to build a relationship, get to know your buyer so you can connect on a human level, rather than just seller and buyer. In the early days of a startup, most customers are taking a risk to give you a try. Getting them on board with your whole story and reason for being is just as important as getting them to buy your product. They can become strong advocates for you. Emotional pull is a powerful part of selling.

TAKE ACTION: CREATE YOUR FULL-LENGTH PITCH DECK

Time to get busy! Let's build a pitch deck.

- Take a stack of index cards or blank sheets of paper (Post-It notes can work too if you want to work on a wall). Each card or page will represent a slide. Write on the top of each what title would go on that slide. Refer back to the list I shared at the beginning of this chapter to help you organize the slides.
- Write one idea that goes with the title of what that slide is about, just a bullet to capture the idea. You should be looking at the 4H Framework flow you did in the last chapter for things you want to be sure you communicate in the story you will tell.
- Spread all those sheets of paper out on a table so you can move them around. Try out a few different orders until you feel like you have it, while still keeping with the 4H Framework flow.
- Now, slide by slide, decide what image, graphic, chart, data, or text would need to go on each slide to best articulate or represent that one idea. You may not yet have that exact graphic or data, and this is okay. Just write down the specific type of information you want to include on each slide. For example, you may make a note on a relevant slide that you will be inserting a four-step process laid out with an icon representing each step. Be as specific as possible so this will help guide your research for icons.
- Step back and assess how it feels. Does it follow your talk track flow? Is there a story arc?
- Choose your platform for creating the deck. Now would be

a good time to check out the templates mentioned in the design section of this chapter.

- Begin finding the graphics you need and designing your slides.

CHAPTER 4

———

Short Pitches With Powerful Punches

David peels off his coffee-stained shirt to reveal another bright white shirt underneath. He then spills the coffee on himself again, but this time, instead of soaking his shirt fabric, the black liquid beads up and rolls off with a swipe of his hand.

The Sharks gasp again, but this time in delighted disbelief. The second shirt, David explains, has been treated with Detrapel, a nanotech-based, super hydrophobic, spray that repels almost any liquid from almost any fabric or surface, protecting them from stains.

David moves into the pitch for his company and his invention, an environmentally friendly and non-toxic—David's co-presenter squirts a good amount into his mouth and swallows it to prove that point—patented stain repellant that has consumer, retail, and industrial uses.

David has been preparing for this moment since he invented Detrapel in high school. He knows the key to a winning pitch in front of the cameras and investor celebrities on ABC's *Shark Tank* is brevity mixed with drama. He needs to show them, as well as tell them, what he and his business are all about. Being confident helps, but so does engaging with the Sharks so they can get to know him.

He demos his product for the Sharks several more times, spilling other substances and liquids on other surface types, capturing their attention. Barbara Corcoran wants to see up close. While standing next to him and examining his shirt, instinctively she fixes his collar. Connection established. He has nailed it on the sense of humor front, and he shows that his product works. He hits his value proposition hard: unlike the competition, Detrapel is completely natural and non-toxic. The Sharks eat it up.

David continues with his pitch, going for buy-in to his bigger vision: a chemical company with a line of products all based on nanotechnology. This is what he needs the Sharks' help for. This is the business that can make him rich and the Sharks richer.

David has established his credibility; he has a very special product and a big market to conquer. He handles their questions about the business with ease, professionally and honestly. Not one, not two, but all five Sharks put out an offer to David. They all want a piece of Detrapel and to work with him to make it successful. He's smiling, enjoying the moment, and staying relaxed but alert for the best deal. He finally accepts Mark Cuban and Lori Grenier's offer, which is what he wanted all along. He leaves the Tank with an opportunity to have high-profile business partners. Millions of people have seen what his company is all about. The effects of David's *Shark Tank* appearance will last for months and allow him to keep building Detrapel.

One of the most amazing aspects of David's Shark Tank pitch was how much he had to pack into a short amount of time. While the rest of the show is certainly edited for time and television viewer appeal, the two-minute opening pitch is, reportedly, sink or swim. Contestants are not given do-overs. Those two minutes are all they get to convince the sharks that there is a problem, that they have solved it, and that their value proposition is worthy of investment.

While the odds of making it to Shark Tank to pitch your startup are slim—*USA Today* reports that each season 40,000 entrepreneurs vie for 88 slots that actually air[9]—you are going to confront plenty of other instances where you need to pare down that full-length pitch to an extremely concise one. Your goal is to convey enough information to pique investor interest and, hopefully, get a second meeting.

Saying a lot in a short period of time can take as much or more energy, thought, and prep-time as a full-length pitch.

There is a famous quote attributed to Mark Twain: *If I had more time I would have written you a shorter letter.* What this quote refers to is how difficult it is to write with brevity, while still making your most salient points.

The two main types of "short" pitches entrepreneurs need to nail are the twenty-to-thirty-second elevator pitch and what we at Babson call the three-minute "rocket pitch." These two pitches are as hard to write and to get right as Twain's short letter.

Because the time limits are so short, every single word in an elevator or rocket pitch must be chosen with care. The good news is that if you nail these short pitches, you'll be more inclined to talk about your pitch to anyone who will listen. And that's a sure-fire

---

9   Gary Levi, "'Shark Tank': All your burning questions, answered," *USA TODAY* , January 7, 2019, https://www.usatoday.com/story/life/tv/2019/01/04/we-answer-your-shark-tank-burning-questions/2463620002/.

way to find all kinds of help for your startup. We will discuss both short pitches in detail in this chapter.

There's another short but vital pitch-related tool that we cover in this chapter, the one-page Executive Summary. This is a pre-pitch document designed as a door-opener to a first meeting, so it too must communicate in a succinct and engaging manner.

ELEVATOR PITCH FRAMEWORK

Most people have at least some idea of what an elevator pitch is supposed to be.

It's the way to spark a conversation with the investor you just happen to be standing in front of in the buffet line at that important networking event. It's what you want to say to the girl you had a crush on all through high school at your ten-year reunion, to make sure she gets that you are now a brilliant entrepreneur (her loss). It's what you are going to say to knock the socks off the guy sitting next to you on the airplane when he asks you, in a polite but disinterested manner, what you do.

In common business vernacular, an elevator pitch is a statement of what your business does, followed by an expression of its unique value proposition, how it solves a problem for the target consumer in a way that is special. In keeping with the idea that you should be able to deliver said pitch in the time it takes an elevator to move up or down a couple of floors, you need to be able to get all the words out in an intelligible manner, ideally in twenty to thirty seconds.

Your elevator pitch must cover what your business does and why in a way that encourages listeners to look up from their phones, lean in, and ask to hear more. You want your elevator pitch to be the first phrase in a long and hopefully fruitful conversation. This is the sole purpose: to get someone to ask the next question.

Creating an elevator pitch is hard work. It cannot come off as scripted, even though you will probably spend a substantial amount of time constructing the perfect lines. Although preceded by serious thought and practice, your elevator pitch needs to appear as natural to you as breathing.

As with so many aspects of new venture communication, my approach is to take a lesson from the best practices of brand marketing.

POSITIONING STATEMENT AS STRUCTURE FOR AN ELEVATOR PITCH

Positioning statements that consumer packaged goods (CPG) marketers use work extremely well as the basis for an elevator pitch. Positioning statements force CPG marketers to differentiate their product from the competition by clearly defining the target customer and then articulating a unique value proposition. An elevator pitch also does this, which is why I recommend starting with the following positioning statement template to create your elevator pitch:

For a **[target customer]** who has **[customer need]**, **[product name]** is a **[market category]** that is **[one key benefit]**. Unlike **[competition]** the product **[unique value proposition]**.

You'll notice that the first blank to fill in is the target customer, something that can be tricky for an early-stage startup.

Finding the right product-market fit is a big milestone for a young company. Investors have a keen interest in seeing how and when you achieve this milestone. They know you need to understand your market inside and out in order to find it.

To dig into your target market, you need more than demographics about ideal customers. You will need to understand customer interests, behaviors, attitudes, attributes, and characteristics sometimes referred to as psychographics.

The most basic definition of psychographics is "things they like." Maybe it's talking about politics, or plant-based foods, or modern design. You can get insight into your customers' psychographics by interviewing or surveying them (or both), and seeing what kinds of themes emerge from a group of people that you hypothesize are your ideal customer. This works for B2B companies as well, and may include such inquiries as looking at how they position themselves in their industry or the incentive structures for your buyer. With this knowledge, you can paint a detailed picture in very few words of exactly who your product is for and why.

Next, you must be able to isolate your customer's need and tie it to the solution you are offering, all the while differentiating yourself from the competition.

As you can see, there is an art to creating a knock-'em-dead elevator pitch. It takes more effort than just filling in the blanks of a positioning statement. You need to express all the elements of a positioning statement without using any jargon. It's harder than it seems. You must provide a frame so the person you're speaking to can quickly catch on to the idea of your startup. By the time you've finished your elevator pitch, the listener's brain should be firing enough synapses to start getting excited without becoming overwhelmed by information they can't possibly grasp in twenty seconds.

To develop a feel for the flow of a positioning statement and how to incorporate it into a winning elevator pitch, take a look at the following examples of well-known companies I'm pitching, and try to imagine that you know nothing about them.

JetBlue Mock Elevator Pitch

JetBlue is an airline whose advertising makes fun of how awful, frustrating, and humorless flying usually is. If I were pitching my new company JetBlue to potential investors, I might say something like:

> For travelers who don't take themselves too seriously but want to fly comfortably and enjoy their time in the air, JetBlue is an airline that understands customer needs to enjoy flying. Unlike other airlines, JetBlue has a sense of humor and makes customers comfortable and happy while they're in the air. You have your own TV, unlimited snacks, and flight attendants and pilots who like to delight passengers with excellent service.

Notice how I am using more descriptive words about the target customer, not details about their age or gender. "Who don't take themselves too seriously" works much more effectively to paint a picture of the ideal customer.

Starbucks Mock Elevator Pitch

Starbucks specialty coffee shops focus on the café experience. I might pitch Starbucks this way:

> For the coffee lover who wants to enjoy a delicious cup of coffee in a comfortable environment, Starbucks is the perfect premium coffee store because it delivers a connected, community-based, retail experience. Unlike a typical coffee shop, Starbucks understands what the coffee culture café experience should be. With amenities like newspapers, high-end food, free Wi-Fi, and music, Starbucks offers more than a place to drink coffee: a place where people want to gather and linger.

Here, I am talking about my target customer as a "coffee lover," but this is a very special kind of coffee lover who wants a café experience. Also, for this pitch I've created an image of my unique value proposition through the way I describe the amenities; and starting with the phrase "Unlike a typical coffee shop," you immediately understand how this is a completely different experience.

BUILD UP YOUR PITCH IN STAGES AND MAKE IT YOUR OWN

Sometimes it can be easier if you develop your elevator pitch in stages. Try doing a first round focused exclusively on describing the target customer followed by a problem-solution statement: what's their need or pain point and how you will fix it.

Find that one sentence to capture the magic of what you are building and for whom. Build in your emotional hook. You don't want to leave out this important piece connecting your unique value proposition. Keep in mind the benefit or solution is not what you do; rather, it's how you do it. Often this can be told using emotion-laden words.

Sometimes people feel more comfortable starting their problem statement in the elevator pitch by saying "We help" or "We increase (or reduce)" something related to the problem. While I don't think this is necessarily the best way to kick off an elevator speech, as it's a little on the plain-sounding side, if you find that starting this way makes it easier to fashion a good pitch, go for it.

After you've nailed the target customer and problem-solution statement, you can layer on the other elements in the pitch, like your place in the category or competition, for instance stating how you are "unlike" others. If you are starting to feel confident with this, you can even bring in how you make money in a tight compelling phrase or sentence. For example, you could say, *We take ten percent of each transaction,* or *We have, on average, eighty percent margins on each purchase.* This can be the "boom" that makes your listener perk up.

For timing and emphasis, I suggest a four-five-six structure: four seconds for the target, five seconds for the problem, six seconds for the solution, filling the remaining time with other persuasive or unique things to note about your startup.

I recommend that you practice your elevator pitch over and over. Tell it to anyone who will listen, and see if they immediately get it. Ideally, you will run it by people who know nothing about what you are doing, so you can rest assured that if they understand it, then you've done a good job communicating without confusing. As I mentioned before, this sentence should come out of your mouth completely naturally and not sound at all stilted or scripted. Ideally, you will know your elevator pitch so well that it just becomes part of how you introduce yourself.

As was the case with the 4H Framework for the full-length pitch, you may find that the order of things in the positioning statement/ elevator pitch template provided above doesn't flow naturally for you. If so, definitely reorder it! The most important thing is that your elevator pitch makes sense and feels comfortable for you. You are the expert on your business, and ultimately you will know what is best. If you want to get started on your elevator pitch, jump to the "Take Action" exercise I offer at the end of this chapter.

If you've got a minute or two longer to get your point across than is normally available for an elevator pitch, consider the slightly expanded rocket pitch.

THE ROCKET PITCH

As mentioned in chapter 1 when I introduced Ravish Majithia and his business Magnomer, we have an event each year at Babson called Rocket Pitch. Each participant is allowed three minutes and three slides, and the goal is to develop a short pitch to convey in a tight, compelling way the key things someone might want to know about your company.

While a rocket pitch is a bit longer than an elevator pitch, you'd be surprised how fast those three minutes fly by. Nailing your rocket pitch can be a big confidence boost, as well as another way to talk about your startup in certain situations and make the most of the airtime.

Generically speaking, a pitch that lasts less than five minutes, whether in a competition or a personal meeting, can be considered a type of rocket pitch. Like the elevator pitch, the purpose of a rocket pitch is to generate enough interest to get the next meeting or engage in a conversation.

A rocket pitch doesn't allow for a ton of information. At a minimum, however, I tell my students entering the Babson Rocket Pitch that they need to answer these four categories of questions, along with presenting their problem–solution statement:

1. What is the **target market**? How big is it now and is it growing? Is there a certain segment of the market that you're keying into first or that you think is underserved for some reason?
2. What is your **unique value proposition**? What differentiates you from the competition? Why now?
3. What are your revenue streams? Or **how do you make money**?
4. Who will be on **your team**? Why are they uniquely able to bring this idea to life?

As I mentioned previously, often with early-stage startups, investors place greater emphasis on characteristics of the founders they invest in than on the business idea. They know from experience that the idea is going to change and reshape as the entrepreneur goes forward in their journey, learns more, and works the process. Introducing your team in your three-minute pitch tells investors who's behind the innovation and why they are uniquely able to execute. The stronger this part of your pitch is, the better, because it can move someone from being mildly interested to being extremely interested.

Before Mighty Well founder Emily Levy entered the Breakaway Pitch Competition, she had shared her vision for her startup at Rocket Pitch. It was her first public pitch about Mighty Well, which was then called PICCPerfect. The Rocket Pitch experience gave her confidence about moving forward with her idea. It also allowed her to hone her three-minute pitch so tightly that eventually she could answer every one of the four question categories in a clear and compelling way.

From her Rocket Pitch presentation, we knew Emily had a robust target market of people who suffer from a chronic illness. We knew her patented line of adaptive wear was like nothing else on the market, and that she had identified how to bring her invention to people who needed her solutions. Finally and perhaps most importantly, we could tell that this spirited young woman, who had already overcome so much found personal empowerment in a very serious medical condition, would be able to deliver on her vision. We knew Emily and her team could change how chronically ill people were perceived by others and how they felt about themselves.

THE EXECUTIVE SUMMARY

The executive summary is another element of pitching that tracks back to the marketing world. It is a well-written, one- or two-page document (front and back) that summarizes the problem your target market is experiencing, the solution you have created, and your business model telling how you make money and how you acquire customers.

Spending the time to get your executive summary just right is vitally important. While its intended purpose is to get an investor interested enough in you and your business to allow you to make a formal pitch, a confusing or poorly written document can have the opposite effect. Investors see hundreds of executive summaries each year. You need to make yours stand out in the best way possible.

While typically used to generate interest to help get a meeting, some entrepreneurs send an executive summary in advance of a scheduled meeting to give the potential investor or mentor a good overview so they can come to the meeting prepared.

Entrepreneurs also send executive summaries to people they hope will make connections for them. A best practice is to attach the executive summary to an introductory email to make it easy for another person to share salient facts about your company without having to draft all the details into an email themselves. This way they know how you want to talk about your business and can stay focused on messages you want to emphasize in the introduction.

In general, an executive summary is written in prose using full paragraphs. You might include a few bullets or section heads. It should be created like a piece of marketing collateral with nicely formatted columns of text, maybe a sidebar, and one or two well-designed graphs. Unlike for your pitch deck, you won't be there to talk through the sheet as your audience reads it, so it needs to stand alone. The sidebar can contain some key statistics or facts about the company such as contact information, founding year, cash burn rate, number of employees, monthly revenue, stage of venture, funding ask, use of funds, and information about any existing investors or relevant industry advisors.

Use any images or graphs judiciously, and only to support key points. Think of the executive summary as a bite-sized business plan. It would usually contain many of the same sections as your pitch deck, where each section gets roughly three to four sentences. As with the pitch deck, avoid acronyms and industry jargon. Each sentence needs to work hard for you and be very direct. Don't waste words on things that don't add value to your story. It needs to be clear, concise, and compelling. Include these sections:

- Problem
- Solution (and why now, if timing plays a role)
- Unique value proposition (competitive advantage)
- Traction (if any)
- Market
- Business model
- Key metrics
- Team
- Ask (optional, this could be how much you are raising)

You'll want to have some commentary on each of these items. If you have impressive traction already or some "value creator" like a patent, intellectual property, a marquis partnership or client, make sure this gets mentioned early on. Begin with an overview to describe the current situation and problem. Like other pitch language we've discussed, this needs to grab their attention. But you won't have the space to tell a story as you do in a live pitch format. It should set the context for what they are about to read in a way that makes them curious to keep reading but is professional. It could be different from your live pitch story. Move quickly to your solution and any competitive advantages you have. As you talk about each section, try to provide just enough detail to give the idea without going down a rabbit hole.

There are Word and other online templates you can find by searching the internet or my website, thefirstpitchbook.com, for help to design your executive summary. If you are not proficient with document design, ask a competent friend or hire a designer—they are available at minimal cost—to format it for you. Your executive summary needs to look amazing, not like your college resume.

When it's done, share it with members of your team and also with people who know nothing about your business. Ask for their feedback to learn whether it's doing its job.

Example of an Executive Summary Layout

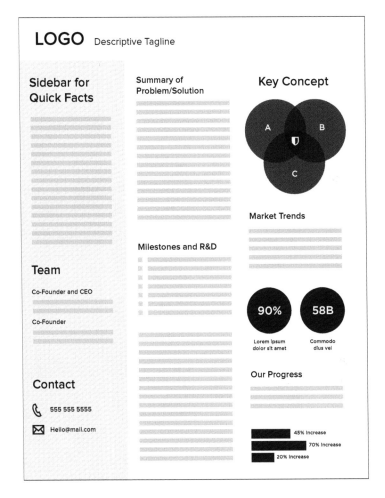

See more examples at TheFirstPitchBook.com

As I mentioned, often this piece will be an attachment to an email that's going to a potential investor or mentor. While you don't need to customize every version of the executive summary, you do need to customize the email you send it with.

As discussed later in more detail, it's important to thoroughly research the people you contact. Where appropriate, leverage any information concerning common areas of interest, people you both know, companies either of you has worked with before, and expertise your recipient is known for in your cover email. This shows you did your due diligence before reaching out, and that you are certain they would be an excellent person to work with. This email should be brief and to the point. You should include your elevator pitch in the body, but the attached executive summary will take care of the rest. Also, be clear about why you are emailing them by stating your ask and how you will follow up. Your goal is to persuade them to take the next step and open the attachment, so don't be afraid to add some light humor or personality to your cover email. But don't say anything silly or overly familiar (e.g., *hey how's your mom feeling?*) if you haven't met them before.

Since this executive summary is going with an email, it helps if you have some kind of email tracking software connected to your email account. It's helpful for your process to know who has opened your emails and read them. If you find they haven't read your email, you may need to try to reach them a different way. And remember to update the executive summary as major milestones are reached or when there are significant changes to the business.

Whether you are presenting a full-length pitch, a rocket pitch, an elevator pitch, or one of the myriad hybrids of these, at some point you want the pitch to transform into a dialogue. You want your audience to show curiosity and interest by asking questions, and you must be prepared to answer without being defensive or indecisive.

Now that you have the tools to create high impact content for your pitch deck, it's time to consider how to wrap your presentation in a visually appealing package. Chapter 5 is all about visual design.

TAKE ACTION: DEVELOP YOUR ELEVATOR PITCH

Time to work on your elevator pitch. Nailing this feels really good so don't delay!

Start by thinking of creative, poignant, intriguing, and/or exciting ways to express or relay each of the following concepts from the template at the beginning of the chapter, one at a time:

- Target customer: use descriptive words or behaviors, not demographics.
- Customer need: use a phrase to describe the problem your customers have and tap into their emotions.
- Product name: what's your idea called? (This one's easy!)
- Market category: if you were putting your solution on a map, what would the map be about? Is this a category that already exists, or are you creating a new one?
- One key benefit: how does it make the target customer feel? What does it help them do? (Some emotions or words that convey emotion work well here too.)
- Competition: isolate a general term for the competition and relate it to the market category.
- Unique value proposition: what is your unique differentiator or secret sauce?

Now, using the positioning statement below, fill in the blanks with the words or phrases that you came up with, changing the wording where necessary so it works with the statement format.

For a **[target customer]** who has **[customer need]**, **[product name]** is a **[market category]** that is **[one key benefit]**. Unlike **[competition]** the product **[unique value proposition]**.

Once you feel like you've done a good job filling in each blank, practice it to see if the order works for you. As long as you cover the relevant concepts, it doesn't matter what sequence you put them in. I will say, though, that it's often easiest to start with the target customer to develop at least the first couple of drafts of your elevator pitch. As you get more comfortable with it, you might shorten it, make it into two or three sentences, or change the phrasing slightly. What's important is that it sounds authentic to you and is easy for you to say.

CHAPTER 5

———

Design Matters

PASSION MEETS DESIGN

The entrepreneurs who created Teplo wanted to capture the ancient art of brewing tea in both the look and feel of their product and their pitch.

Mayuresh Soni and Kazu Kawanobi are both from tea-drinking countries in Southeast Asia, where brewing and drinking tea is a centuries-old tradition full of beauty and meaning. To bring an exciting, modern twist to this tradition, they created Teplo, a "smart" tea kettle that you can connect to an app on your phone.

Beautifully crafted teas and an artfully designed kettle are integral to the Teplo experience. The company's unique value proposition aims to create the delightful experience tea drinkers expect from perfectly brewed tea, adding a special moment to the day. Their pitch deck needed to reflect a design aesthetic embracing the concept of something beautifully crafted and delightful to use.

They did not disappoint. They designed an app to transport the user visually: images of loose leaf teas from around the world, colorful and textured; video of a seamless, serene user experience showing the fine art of tea brewing with a technical twist, a message totally consistent with Teplo's brand.

The minimalist images brightened with colorful dried flowers surrounded by modern glass accessories perfectly complemented each other, allowing the radiance of the tea to shine through. The mood was modern, yet sublime, a perfect way to showcase a product combining an ancient art with modern technology.

The pitch deck made beautiful use of white space, effectively highlighting the story's main ideas, incorporating pictures to enhance the message, using a clear, simple, modern font to create just the right mood.

Investors viewing the deck could immediately sense that these entrepreneurs understood design, something critical for success with a hardware product. Also apparent was their ability to harness the power of their brand to tell a story that would resonate with all who appreciate the tea-drinking experience.

Appearances matter in pitching. Whether you are pitching one-on-one, one-to-several, or one-to-thousands, how your pitch deck comes across from an aesthetic point of view can make or break a presentation. People make snap judgments; and once a person's mind is set, it can be difficult to walk back a first impression.

Think about the visual design of your deck as the wrapper for your content. It needs to reflect the image you hope to project while also supporting your main messages.

Good design begins with attention to detail. If your pitch deck looks sloppy, or if it has spelling errors, typos, or overcrowded slides, people subjectively make the leap that you, and by extension your whole operation, are sloppy. What else don't you care about? What details of building your company, executing on deliverables, or protecting their investment are you going to overlook? Nobody wants a sloppy business associate. Fortunately, there are tried-and-true rules you can follow to help create a well-designed presentation.

RULES FOR WELL-DESIGNED PRESENTATIONS

As the story about Teplo shows, when the look of the deck aligns with the message and the company, you are bound to make a favorable impression. In order to achieve good design, there are certain rules that, with few exceptions, should always be followed. These universal rules for successful presentations are worth committing to memory:

- White space is your friend. Don't have a lot of clutter; stick to one idea per slide. (Litmus test: can you read the slide from far away?)
- Use the same font on every slide (but never use Comic Sans)
- Use a font that makes sense for the aesthetic you are going for (as long as it's not Comic Sans)

- Make sure the images you use match the aesthetic you want to achieve
- Make the style consistent throughout the whole deck

This example from Teplo's deck beautifully explains how their product works while adhering to the design rules outlined above.

Courtesy of Kazunori Kawanobe and Mayuresh Soni | Load-Road Inc.

Many people use PowerPoint for a presentation deck, but it does have limitations. Fortunately, several companies have created excellent templates that are usable in PowerPoint. They're drag-and-drop, and the companies have already thought through visual presentation rules to help you craft something that fits, providing a wonderful jumpstart to your presentation and saving you from the agony of staring at a blank page. The different slide templates incorporate various structures and formats to help you tell your story in a clear way.

Canva and Slidebean are two examples of sites that offer free templates you can download and use to fill in your own content. They offer even a novice the opportunity to create a professional look. You can also go to graphic design marketplaces like 99designs or Fiverr and put your job out to professional designers all over the world to bid on, yet another benefit of the gig economy, and decide from there which partner you want to work with.

THE USE OF IMAGERY

Let me start with this: Using clip art on a PowerPoint is a sure-fire way to ruin a pitch deck. Do not use it. Ever.

The graphics should all be consistent in style. If your company is modern and sexy, you want to use modern and sexy graphics. Great imagery is memorable.

Sometimes you can use the image to help people remember things you want them to remember. For example, Ravish uses a shock and awe tactic with his graphics when pitching his magnetic ink company. He introduces photos of huge piles of plastic on beaches. This is profoundly disturbing. Then he shows a picture of plastic with magnetic ink on it being moved to recycling, and that's memorable. Actual photographs can deliver impact.

If you find that you need to use stock images, that's okay, as long as they are beautiful and stylized. There are plenty of sources for free photographs, so be careful that you don't use copyrighted material without permission. Inadvertently misappropriating intellectual property never makes a good impression in a pitch.

Use images and photographs that render well both on screen and printed; they'll need to be high resolution so they don't look fuzzy or hard to read. The site startupstockphotos.com provides nice stock footage for PowerPoint decks. Another, unsplash.com, has inexpensive, high-quality images that are not copyright-protected. It is worth buying nice graphics for your pitch deck; it can make all the difference.

Icons make a deck look modern and clean. They convey an idea via a symbol. If you use icons on a slide, make sure they are all from the same family and stick to that styling throughout the presentation. For example, if one is in blue and reflects a certain style, they should all be in blue in that certain style. Also, emojis are not icons. Do not confuse them with icons, and do not use them.

A company called The Noun Project provides many free, low-cost icons that can be used in pitch decks. Icons look simple, convey a lot, and help reinforce your message if used consistently.

A WORD ABOUT LOGOS

Touching back to the marketing world again, your logo represents a key element of your brand meaning.

Your logo is an integral part of your company persona. It's your company's visual signature. It signals what your company stands for, what its personality is, and those you hope it will attract. It may be just one piece of your branding, but it is a very important one.

Your logo can create emotion for a consumer just by virtue of its design.

Design elements, including colors and fonts you use and the feelings they evoke, provide a first impression of your company. I strongly suggest you consider getting a logo professionally designed if possible. An amateur-looking logo can derail the image you are trying to create for your startup. Commissioning a logo doesn't have to be an expensive endeavor; there are several sites where you can get an original logo design for $100 to $200.

A few tips for logo-design best practices:

- Your logo should be simple. It should not make people feel like they need to stare at it for a while to get it.
- It should look good in either black and white or color, and it should be scalable. In other words, it should look good whether it is tiny (printed on a pen) or large (printed on a billboard).
- Any text used in your logo should be kept to a minimum.

There are **six** key design types for logos, according to DesignHill.[10]

1. **Letter marks** are created in the form of initials of a company name using creative typography. Think IBM or NASA.
2. **Wordmarks** are similar to letter mark designs but use fonts to represent a company name in an original way. Think Coca-Cola.
3. **Logo symbols** use a picture or symbol to create a brand personality that is recognizable by the symbol alone. Think Twitter, Target, and Apple.
4. **Abstract logo marks** are image-based but use an abstract

---

10 Eshley Jackson, "Different Types of Logo Design For Your Business," *designhill,* https://www.designhill.com/design-blog/different-types-of-logo-design-for-your-business/.

graphic as a symbol for what the product stands for. Think Nike.

5. **Mascot logos** use a character or person created to represent the brand. Think KFC.

6. **Combination logos** combine two types of logo styles, maybe a picture and a wordmark or a mascot and a wordmark in such a way that the text and the picture are molded together or shown side by side. Think Burger King.

Once you have come up with a logo design, you will need to decide how best to use it in your pitch deck. Conventional wisdom says that entrepreneurs should always have their logos on their cover slides. Whether or not to feature a logo on each subsequent slide, however, is up to each presenter. I'm in favor of including a logo on every slide if it's not too distracting from the overall feel of the deck. The point is to leverage your logo to help support the brand story you are telling in your pitch.

We have covered how to create content for pitches, and pitch decks of all types and lengths, and how to wrap them in an attractive design package. Now it's time to work on pitch delivery. The next chapter will address the most important interpersonal skills and behaviors you need to master in order to come across as a thoughtful and open potential partner.

TAKE ACTION: DEVELOP YOUR CREATIVE BRIEF

When putting together your pitch deck, you will be thinking about design elements and how they help convey your company's image. This is a good time to consider putting together your company's creative brief to help internal or outsourced designers create consistent, market-facing materials and visual communications for your startup.

The purpose of a creative brief is to help a designer develop materials for your brand that are consistent with what you are trying to communicate to the world. A creative brief includes specific design elements and vital information about your company, such as your position in the market and your target customer, to help designers translate your brand into visual cues and images.

Going through the steps of analyzing your company from the perspective of developing a creative brief forces you to dig even deeper to learn more about your customers, sharpen your value proposition, and identify what you stand for. You will need to present these concepts and business elements to your designer so they have a deep enough understanding of your company to create materials that speak to the audiences you are trying to reach.

A creative brief doesn't have to be fancy. The important thing is that it guides design work so that the output is a visual reflection of the company you are building. You can start to develop your creative brief by answering some key questions:

Project Description: What are you asking the creative professional to design?

Communication Objective: What is the goal for this piece? What do you hope it will do for you? For example: Do you want it to drive awareness or trial? Create excitement for a launch? Generate interest from investors?

Target Audience: Who is the target audience? What are their demographics and psychographics?

Key Insight: What will motivate this audience?

Key Benefit/Unique Value Proposition: What is your unique value proposition? What functional, emotional, or social need does your product or service fill for the customer?

Support Points: What makes this message about your company believable? What are some reasons, or key features or functions of your product, that will make your target market believe in your product or service?

Desired Response: What response do you hope to get from this communication? What do you want the customer to do?

Personality Characteristics/Style and Tone: If your company were a person, what words would you use to describe it? For example, would you say that it's modern, fun, helpful, caring, authoritative, or intellectual?

Comparables: Are there websites or other creative designs that you think capture what you want your own communication to look like? Is there a mood you're going for that's captured in an image? If so, provide website URLs, photos, or other images as examples.

Must-Haves: Are there any required elements to this communication? For example, do you need to include a regulatory disclosure or a source credit?

Please Don't: Is there anything the creative should definitely avoid doing?

Due Date and Formats: What is the due date for the final work? What format should it be delivered in?

CHAPTER 6

———

Interpersonal Dynamics in Pitching

THE IMPORTANCE OF BEING AUTHENTIC

Renowned seed-stage investor, mentor, and Stanford University dSchool instructor Michael Dearing knows how to ask all the right questions. In order to get to the root of a particular startup or business model, he lets founders relax into their pitch, hoping their personalities and "special sauce" that distinguishes their startup or business model will shine through.

Every so often, Michael has told me, he is taken completely by surprise by what that special sauce is and how it manifests itself in early-startup entrepreneurs and others.

Michael tells a story about a team of founders who, on the surface, didn't seem like they could make the grade. Inexperienced and unpolished, the two young men delivered to Michael in his Silicon Valley office a pitch that needed work. Even though their pitch was stiff and uninspiring, Michael instinctively felt these guys had something worth pursuing, so he started to dig.

As he asked question after question, he became increasingly impressed with the young founders and their answers. "They were eleven out of ten of their best selves once we got into the conversation," he said, adding that the young entrepreneurs were clear and forthcoming about the risks inherent in their model, detailing deficiencies and sharing thoughtful insights on what they planned to do about them. They listened to criticism, taking it in stride, then jumping ahead to explain how they planned to make their product and their business better.

"It's totally appropriate at this stage for there to be uncertainty on various elements, and it's okay to admit what you don't know," Michael said.

Michael appreciated how the two handled his no-holds-barred questioning. Instead of taking the problem Michael uncovered as a "fatal flaw," the founders showed themselves as thoughtful, creative, problem-solvers who were honest and transparent.

As it turned out, the one thing that could have brought down their idea ended up revealing their positive attitude and sound thought process, as well as openness and transparency that Michael found compelling. Based on this, he shared his network to help them on their fundraising journey, a huge win for the young startup entrepreneurs.

So far, we've covered how to put together different types of pitches supported by compelling talk tracks and flawlessly designed pitch decks. But well-practiced pitches are not enough. If you want to pitch like a pro, you must bring more to the table. Like the young entrepreneurs who impressed Michael Dearing, you are going to have to bring your authentic, open, approachable, best self. While Michael did not invest with the young men, he came away with a favorable enough impression to help them nonetheless.

It's important to remember that you are in this for the long haul. If something doesn't work out exactly as planned in a meeting, you still want to leave behind a good impression. You never know who might take a special interest in you and your company. People generally do want to be helpful to entrepreneurs if they can.

This is why it is so important to recognize that a pitch is more than a way to get people to invest in your company. The pitch is your opportunity to show who you are as a founder and what it might be like to work with you. Jamie Goldstein, a twenty-year veteran in venture capital and the founder of Pillar VC, says that when he sits down with an entrepreneur, the first thing he wants to know is their life story. He doesn't want to hear about their target market or look at their P&L or delve into dollars and cents issues that, eventually, he is going to want to understand. Jamie wants to know the person sitting in front of him. He feels strongly that the more he knows about the entrepreneur's personal story, the background beyond the resume, the better he can gauge what type of founder they will be. He wants to work with founders who will "blow through walls, are relentlessly curious and self-aware, strategic, and have that 'it' factor to create a movement around their startup."

CRUSH THE Q&A

In most pitch scenarios, the best way for potential investors to see the entrepreneur's authentic personality, how they think and what they are made of, is during the question and answer session. This is where how you react and respond to questions can make or break your chances to get to the next level.

Most of the time, the Q&A occurs after you've gone through your full pitch and have opened the floor for questions. The only constant with the Q&A is that it will be different every time. You need to be good on your feet, stay focused, and provide thoughtful answers. Investors and mentors often use the Q&A session to test how you operate under pressure or when you are given negative feedback. The unscripted moments show them what you as an entrepreneur are made of.

Of course, there will be times when your formal pitch is interrupted by questions from investors or mentors. While this may take you off your perfectly planned and rehearsed flow, count your blessings if this happens. The quicker you can get into a conversation with an investor the better. Any opportunity you get to show your real interpersonal qualities and how you think will help an investor gain understanding of the full picture and the opportunity you are presenting.

What is it exactly that investors are looking for in a founder? Skills and experience are obviously important, but less tangible personal and relational factors also play an important role. Studies show, for example, that entrepreneurs who are perceived as trustworthy are more likely to receive investment offers.[11]

COACHABILITY COUNTS

Angel investors want to back early-stage entrepreneurs they can mentor. Many investors believe their time and expertise is as valuable as their money, so they want to invest in companies where their personal involvement can have an impact. This means looking for entrepreneurs who are "coachable."

To be coachable means that you are open to feedback, other people's expertise, and new and different ideas that may be relevant

---

11   Maxwell, Andrew L., and Moren Lévesque (2014), "Trustworthiness: A critical ingredient for entrepreneurs seeking investors," *Entrepreneurship Theory and Practice*, 38(5): 1057-1080.

to your startup. Being coachable means you are ready to engage in a deeper way without being defensive. Coachability is one of the biggest components of being perceived as trustworthy.[12] Early-stage investors see their potential expert advisor role as important as, or even more important than, their role as monetary contributor. They want to know that you value the advisory role of their contribution and that you are willing to listen and integrate their feedback into your business decisions.

Research supports the notion that coachability is extremely important to investors. For example, a 2010 study by Northeastern University professor Cheryl Mitteness showed that coachability influences whether an angel investor would recommend moving forward with a company after a pitch.[13] Similarly, in a 2014 study, my Babson colleague Dr. Lakshmi Balachandra found that the more willing an entrepreneur is to accept feedback and engage with suggestions offered during a pitch, the more interested investors are in supporting the company.

Dr. Balachandra's study found that coachability has an impact, regardless of how strongly investors rank a venture's economic fundamentals or the competence of the team. This suggests that cultivating and demonstrating a willingness to learn can give entrepreneurs an extra edge, even if they don't increase their team's skillset or boost the business' cash flow, which can be much more daunting to achieve.

---

12 Balachandra, Lakshmi, Pitching Trustworthiness: Cues for Trust in Early-Stage Investment Decision-Making (August 2, 2011). Available at SSRN: https://ssrn.com/abstract=2205965 or http://dx.doi.org/10.2139/ssrn.2205965.

13 Mitteness, C. R., Sudek, R., & Baucus, M. S. (2010). Entrepreneurs as authentic transformational leaders: critical behaviors for gaining angel capital. Frontiers of Entrepreneurship Research, 30(5), 3.

Other recent research provides additional support. In their study, Professor Matt Marvel from Ball State University and Professor Donald Kuratko from the Kelley School of Business at Indiana University determined that coachability correlates positively with investor interest and willingness to recommend others to invest, and also with a venture's progress toward reaching goals.[14]

BECOMING MORE COACHABLE

If you find you are not a natural when it comes to demonstrating your coachability, if you know you appear defensive even when consciously trying not to, there are steps you can take to improve your communication skills in this regard. In fact, coachability is almost entirely within an entrepreneur's control. While you can't learn to code or add an impressive job to your resume overnight, anyone can try to be more open to advice and mentorship.

Start by genuinely taking an interest in the perspectives of investors. Just showing that you appreciate the experience and advice they offer can go a long way in showing your eagerness to learn. When you are challenged or given feedback, instead of following your instincts to defend yourself, make a point of asking clarifying questions. Probe for more insight in an interested way. And if you still need to work on your coachability skills, you might want to consider taking some tips from the world of improv comedy and learn to say, *yes, and...*

---

14 Marvel, M. R. & Kuratko, D. F (January 2020). Tech Startup Readiness Project Summary Report. Presented at the United States Association of Small Business and Entrepreneurship Conference, New Orleans, LA.

Getting to Yes, and...

A major tenet of improvisational comedy is the *yes, and...* mentality. Because everything in improv is unscripted, actors never know what fellow troupe members are going to say or do. The way they manage to keep the comedic action flowing seamlessly and hilariously is to take whatever their fellow actors say or do and accept it as valid from the get-go. A *yes, and...* mindset is the polar opposite of being defensive.

The "Yes" shows openness to other people's ideas and a sense of cooperation, rather than shutting something down with a "no" or other judgment, which ends the conversation on a down note. The "and" shows that you listened and can build on the idea and steer it in a direction that makes sense for your startup.

For example, when you're in a pitch answering questions or challenges from your audience of mentors or investors, you can demonstrate that you're open to ideas by using declarative agreement phrases like, "I see what you are saying and I agree that..." or "Yes, and another way of expressing that might be..."

Active Listening

Another way to show you are acknowledging and internalizing what others say is through active listening techniques, which are both verbal and non-verbal.

You want to make it clear that you are "seen" as listening to feedback, that you have a genuine interest in what the speaker has to say. You can show this through eye contact, nodding, and even by straightening your posture or leaning forward.

You can also demonstrate active listening by asking clarifying questions and probing for additional insights. Here, in order to show that you heard and understood their point, you begin your response by repeating back the question or statement to the person. For instance, you might truncate or paraphrase what the person said to you and then ask, "Do I have that right?" Then you can feel free to proceed with your answer, having provided validation to the investor that they have been heard.

Both "*yes, and...*" and the active listening approaches demonstrate that you can pivot your thinking when called upon to do so. They suggest that you will keep an open mind not only when working with investors, but when you are leading a team in your company.

FOLLOW UP ON FEEDBACK

Take every opportunity available to demonstrate your coachability, and by all means, if someone imparts wisdom to help your business prosper, pick up a pen and paper and write it down! The questions they ask signal where there are gaps or issues in your pitch.

I can't count the number of times I've witnessed a founder just stand and nod in agreement when a seasoned investor and brilliant businessperson is shelling out the kind of insights that it would take a young startup entrepreneur years to develop on their own. I guarantee the adrenaline rush you experience in that moment makes you think you are taking in all that wisdom, but you're not. You aren't going to remember it and you'll be kicking yourself later. Anticipate these moments, and keep pen and paper ready. Writing down the advice will help you retain it, and it shows the investor in real time that you care about and value what they are saying. It shows that you are indeed coachable.

When you receive useful business feedback, you should not only integrate it into the next conversation you have with a potential investor, but also you should circle back to the investor who gave you the feedback and tell them how valuable it was. If the investor told you to follow up with someone, you should do so and then report back that you took the advice. It's about making sure the investor knows you valued the introduction they made or the piece of advice they gave you.

You'll also get feedback on your deck and the formal part of your pitch. This is useful information because it can help you prepare better for the next meeting.

Eric Paley, Managing Partner of Founder Collective, a top venture capital firm, provides helpful advice for entrepreneurs via his blog (on Medium.com) and on Twitter. Related to the importance of incorporating feedback into your deck, Paley says:

> Be methodical about addressing critiques of the deck. Incorporate pushback into your deck. If a point won't fit in the main flow, build an appendix slide. Every objection should provide data that gets you closer to a "yes."[15]

EMPHASIZE COMPATIBILITY

As an entrepreneur, you need to sell investors on more than your business and your willingness to learn. You also need to show

---

15 https://medium.com/swlh/a-ridiculously-detailed-fundraising-guide-dec6f4f33790.

that you and your business align with the investor's expertise and interests. Investors want protégés they are compatible with, and they want to know they can make a meaningful contribution to an entrepreneur's success.

Don't be afraid to be assertive here. If it's not readily apparent how an investor might help you, call out the connections explicitly and present a vision of how they fit into the success of your business.

FEEDBACK QUALIFIERS

There is an important distinction between listening to all feedback and taking affirmative steps based on that feedback. It is your business, and ultimately, you have to decide if the feedback you receive is relevant and important for you. The idea of being open to it is universal, but being open and listening to feedback does not mean you are *obligated* to follow through with it. If entrepreneurs acted on every single piece of feedback they got without putting their own filter on it, they would bounce around like a pinball in a machine. That's not a good thing.

I talked about this concept with Jeff Avallon. Jeff told me that investors really want to see a founder who is focused and decisive about the way forward. If a founder states in a pitch that he's unsure which of three options to go with, an investor will not feel confident that the entrepreneur has a plan. They want to see you being intentional in your path. He says, "Investors would rather see a founder who can move a ten-pound rock a mile than ten one-pound stones an inch."

When you receive advice that you don't think is right for you, you still need to acknowledge it as valid and appreciate it. However, you should say why it's not the path for you right now and give a solid reason. As with the two entrepreneurs Michael Dearing met in the story that opened this chapter, it is an opportunity to show how you think and to demonstrate leadership, both things investors are evaluating as they speak with you. Being your authentic self is the key; don't just tell them what you think they want to hear. Should this relationship proceed, it is likely to last a long time, and being something you are not will come back to bite you.

A NOTE ABOUT LAUGHTER

One last point about interpersonal skills: it helps to show that you are having fun!

Believe it or not, laughing can affect how you are perceived in the pitch. Returning to Dr. Balachandra's research portfolio on trustworthiness,[16] she analyzed 101 videos of entrepreneurs pitching Tech Coast Angels, a network of early-stage investors in California. She then interviewed the angels post-pitch and reviewed the entrepreneurs' fundraising success, concluding that investor perception of an entrepreneur's character was influenced by "greater laughter by the entrepreneur during the pitch, which led to greater coachability assessments."

"Laughing demonstrates the relative openness of the entrepreneur and the way a future relationship might look with the investor," Dr. Balachandra says. The lesson here is have a little fun in the

---

16   Balachandra, Lakshmi, Pitching Trustworthiness: Cues for Trust in Early-Stage Investment Decision-Making (August 2, 2011). Available at SSRN: https://ssrn.com/abstract=2205965 or http://dx.doi.org/10.2139/ssrn.2205965.

pitch, and don't take yourself too seriously. Don't force laughter; but if there's a genuine moment that is actually funny, don't worry about showing your sense of humor. The investor or mentor wants to see a bit of your personality so they can determine if working with you long-term is going to be a good experience.

TAKE ACTION: PRACTICE YOUR COACHABILITY MINDSET

Get ready for your Q&A session by setting up a practice session.

Make a list of questions that you think might come up about your startup.

Do some research on the people you are presenting to. What further questions might you add, now that you know more about their interests and experience?

Practice with a friend or work partner. Have them ask hard questions and press you so you can get used to being under pressure and staying cool. Ask them to interrupt you and try to throw you off balance so you can practice how you'd handle this in the real situation. Use your active listening techniques to show you are engaged with all your senses.

CHAPTER 7

———

Confronting Bias in the Pitch Process

THE REALITY FOR WOMEN

"It's not something they understand or have ever even thought about."

The topic? Female bladder leakage. The "they" in this quote? Investors, the vast majority of whom are male.

Diane Hessan, investor, serial entrepreneur, and founder of Salient Ventures, was explaining what female founders are often up against, using the example of the early-stage startup named Attn: Grace.

Attn: Grace's women co-founders have plans to upend the women's personal care category, starting with an innovative product to confront bladder leakage, a problem that affects more than 17 million women in the United States alone. With the aging population, this number is expected to grow steadily each year.

The founders' grand plan is to disrupt the industry with an entire range of personal care products to serve women as their bodies age. It's a massive market with plenty of room for innovation. The opportunity is real. But as is often the case, a startup that solves a uniquely female problem has a hard time getting past the first meeting. Most investors, who are male, have no experience with the market and have not wanted to tread into this particular category.

Diane, who has transcended the male-dominated investor world herself and now uses her hard-won knowledge to help other women entrepreneurs find investors, pulled no punches advising these founders how to proceed.

They were going to have to talk about female bladder leakage to a roomful of male investors. There was no way to avoid getting into the details, and it could get, well, awkward.

Diane's advice for the team? Help investors prepare for the meeting by suggesting they talk to their wives about it beforehand.

"If they can come into the meeting having learned from their wives, or other important females in their lives, that this is a real problem without good solutions in the market currently, they will be much more open to the pitch. It's unfortunate that this is how it needs to go, but the fact is that fem-related products have a lot of extra hurdles in order to get the right attention with investors."

To prepare their pitch, Diane tells them to hit the market size and financials hard. The numbers are impressive and have the oversized potential these investors are looking for. The focus should be squarely on the opportunity and the strength of the founding team.

So far, all the advice I've offered for pitch preparation and presentation is universal. All entrepreneurs need to understand storytelling and how to infuse emotion into their pitches to connect with the audience. Everyone needs to develop pitches with some kind of flow, understand how to create compelling pitch decks and other presentation materials, and practice being able to show off knowledge and coachability under stress.

However, the reality is that some things about pitching are biased in favor of white males. Women and minority entrepreneurs may experience the process very differently. Therefore, it is essential that all entrepreneurs learn to recognize and deal with bias in the startup world so they can develop strategies to mitigate it. In this chapter, I discuss this bias as it relates in particular to women, although both women and minority entrepreneurs will find the proposed solutions and work-arounds useful.

LIKE IS ATTRACTED TO LIKE

According to a 2017 *Harvard Business Review* article,[17] female founders receive about two percent of all venture funding, despite owning thirty-eight percent of all businesses in the country. Black

17   https://hbr.org/2017/06/male-and-female-entrepreneurs-get-asked-different-questions-by-vcs-and-it-affects-how-much-funding-they-get.

startup founders received just one percent of U.S. venture capital funding in 2015, despite making up eleven percent of the U.S. population, according to a 2015 CB Insights Analysis.[18]

One reason given for the poor record of investing in female and minority startups is that we need more female and minority investors. In fact, according to the Diana Report from 2014, venture capital firms with women partners are three times more likely to invest in companies with women CEOs.[19]

Investors tend to want to invest in someone like themselves, so if most venture capitalists and investors are white males, they will generally invest in white men. In other words, sometimes investors have expectations about pitches that go beyond the content. When the entrepreneur giving the pitch is "different" from the stereotype of the successful entrepreneur, who is often a white male, this can make it more difficult for an entrepreneur who is a woman or a person of color to convince an investor of the value of their venture. This is a concept called homophily: the usually unconscious tendency for "pattern matching." In other words, we like, trust, and feel more aligned with people like us.

The sociological research that exposes this unconscious thought process is extensive.[20] In categorizing people, the inclination is to

---

18   https://www.cbinsights.com/research/team-blog/venture-capital-diversity-data.

19   Diana Report, *Women Entrepreneurs 2014: Bridging the Gender Gap in Venture Capital*, Professors Candida G. Brush, Patricia G. Greene, Lakshmi Balachandra, and Amy E. Davis. Arthur M. Blank Center for Entrepreneurship, Babson College, September 2014.

20   The Social Psychology of Tokenism: Status and Homophily Processes on Wall Street; Louise Marie Roth, University of Arizona, Sociological Perspectives, Volume 47, Number 2, pages 189-214. Copyright © 2004 by Pacific Sociological Association.

classify first on dimensions that are immediately apparent such as gender and race.[21]

There is no doubt that a more diverse investor population would benefit the investing process and society as a whole. The reality is, however, that the investing community has a long way to go. If you are a woman or minority entrepreneur, you need practical advice on how to level the playing field so your pitch is taken seriously.

My first piece of advice for women and minority founders is to seek funders who focus on these groups and, even better, who have a history of funding them.

My second is to adopt the best practices that we teach at Babson to handle the bias you might confront in a pitch situation.

HANDLING BIAS IN THE Q&A SESSION

In 2017, researchers from Columbia Business School conducted a study on question-and-answer interactions at TechCrunch Disrupt New York City using data from 2010 through 2016.[22] What they found was that venture capitalists, both male and female, tended to ask men more "promotion questions" while they tended to ask women more "prevention questions."

A promotion question is about growth, vision, and opportunity.

---

21   Cecilia L. Ridgeway and Lynn Smith-Lovin, The Gender System and Interaction, *Annual Review of Sociology*, Vol. 25 (1999), pp. 191-216.

22   https://hbr.org/2017/06/male-and-female-entrepreneurs-get-asked-different-questions-by-vcs-and-it-affects-how-much-funding-they-get.

A typical promotion question would be, *what are your plans for growing your business?*

A prevention question is about tactical plans to stave off doom: *how are you going to manage the risk?*

Which kind of question you are asked matters. When asked a promotion question you are likely to respond with a promotion answer. You get to tell the investor all your great plans for growing your company into a successful enterprise. When asked a prevention question, however, you are likely to respond with a prevention answer. You are immediately on the defensive, talking about how you will handle all the negative things that could happen.

The difference is palatable. And what's worse, because you respond to the prevention question with a defensive answer, you are actually giving positive reinforcement to the questioner, unconsciously adding credibility to the line of questioning.

It may seem like a subtle distinction at first, but research shows that the questions asked and answered indeed make a difference in how an entrepreneur is perceived and ultimately funded. According to the Columbia Business School researchers, entrepreneurs who are asked mainly promotion questions raise on average seven times more money than those who are asked mainly prevention questions.[23]

Let's say you are asked, *what are you doing to grow your customer base?* Boom! You can now talk about all your incredible marketing

---

23 Ibid.

and sales activities. But what if instead you are asked, *what are you doing to retain your current customers?* Your answer is now going to focus on your strategy for not losing customers. Positive vs. negative. How to win vs. how not to lose.

Who would you rather put your money on? A winner or a not loser?

EMPOWERING WOMEN TO WIN

At Babson, our CWEL (Center for Women's Entrepreneurial Leadership) female founders' accelerator program, Women Innovating Now Lab or WIN Lab for short, teaches female entrepreneurs how to recognize and respond to prevention and promotion questions.

For example, Susan Duffy, Executive Director of CWEL, explains that when female founders are asked a prevention question, we teach them to move it to a promotion answer by responding to the prevention part quickly and then immediately framing a response that is more about growth and opportunity.

When asked, *how are you going to defend your market share?* we encourage women founders to respond by talking about how much market share growth is anticipated: w*e are confident that we will double our market share in the next two years by bringing two of our pipeline products over the finish line, targeting the valuable seniors market, and adding strategic channel partners.*

We also know that women but hardly ever men are often asked lifestyle questions, such as what their plans are for having children and how they think they would handle juggling career and family.

Again, the advice is to turn the question back to growth and your single-minded determination to make that happen, perhaps saying, *my partner and I have talked about it, but we have no immediate plans. What we're excited about is growing this company.* Or if you are already a mom, give it your badass mom answer: *Parenting makes us all better CEOs. I do more before 8 a.m. than most non-parent entrepreneurs do by noon. My business is as much a part of my family as my kids are. There is nothing that will stop me from seeing them all thrive.*

The goal is to pivot the question you were asked into the question you want to be asked. You can do this by answering in a way that paints the picture that you want the investor to see, one where you are offering them an awesome, investment-worthy opportunity. This tactic, of course, is not limited to questions asked to women. Minority entrepreneurs also can adopt the same tactics in their answers.

Unfortunately, until times change, if you are a female or minority entrepreneur, you will invariably have to address these kinds of questions. Stay calm, keep cool, and know you have the tools to turn it around quickly and impress the investors with an upbeat answer. If an investor continues to track back to lines of questioning such as these after multiple redirects, that investor probably isn't for you. The mental and emotional energy you would need to change this person's thinking probably isn't worth it. Patiently and gracefully get through the meeting and then move on.

SAMPLE PROMOTION VS. PREVENTION QUESTIONS

TOPIC	PROMOTION	PREVENTION
Customers	**Acquisition** "How do you plan to acquire customers?"	**Retention** "How many daily and monthly active users do you have?"
Market	**Size & Growth** "Do you think the target market is a growing one?"	**Share** "Is it a defensible business wherein others can't come into the space and take share?"
Income Statement	**Sales** "How do you plan to monetize this?"	**Margins** "How long will it take you to break even?"
Balance Sheet	**Assets** "How are you leveraging your core assets to grow?"	**Liabilities** "What level of liabilities will be incurred?"
Projections	**Growth** "What major milestones are you targeting for this year?"	**Stability** "How predictable are your future cash flows?"
Strategy	**Vision** "What's the brand vision?"	**Execution** "Are you planning to Turing test this?"

Source: Dana Kanze, Laura Huang, Mark A. Conley and E. Tory Higgins, "Male and Female Entrepreneurs Get Asked Different Questions by VCs — and It Affects How Much Funding They Get," *Harvard Business Review*, June 27, 2017, https://hbr.org/2017/06/male-and-female-entrepreneurs-get-asked-different-questions-by-vcs-and-it-affects-how-much-funding-they-get.

SPECIALIZED MARKETS

Another factor that comes into play is that male investors may not understand certain products that are designed for a women's market sector.

Diane Hessen's pitch story for bladder control products, given at the beginning of this chapter, exemplifies how hard it can be for a pitch audience to know what a founder is talking about. Because male investors do not personally experience or understand the scope of the problem, they have no interest in funding a solution.

A similar example is the case of Cora, providers of tampons and sanitary pads made from organic materials. The now-successful company was eschewed by men who could not see past their aversion to all things menstruation to embrace the huge market potential for these types of products. Businesses that produce other woman-centric items such as for skincare, fashion, maternity, and nursing innovations, often face the same uphill battle.

When pitching companies like these, you may encounter a male investor's attempt to cut your pitch short by remarking that he doesn't understand the product, but he promises to consult with his wife. When that happens, we coach our entrepreneurs to say something like, *yes, ask your wife, but first I can show you what a huge opportunity this is,* and then you launch a conversation about growth.

TAKE ACTION: IDENTIFY PROMOTION
VS. PREVENTION QUESTIONS

- Watch others pitch and see if you can start to identify promotion vs. prevention questions in the Q&A. If you can't get to a pitch competition, watch Shark Tank or another type of pitching show.
- Practice handling prevention questions, and turning them into promotion answers that keep the conversation going in a growth direction.
- Have a few phrases you've practiced repeatedly to help you move into "switch it" mode so you can easily bring it back to growth and the good stuff. Start with something like, *we are confident that...* Just starting a sentence this way can actually make you feel more confident!

CHAPTER 8

Practical Presentation Tips

BUSY BEAUTY

They thought it was just a "meet and greet." Jamie Steen-bakkers and Michael Leahy, co-founders of Busy Beauty, had worked hard to get a meeting with this investor. They were told they had fifteen minutes of his time. He was extremely busy, no time for a pitch. But maybe if they did a good job, they'd get asked back. They wanted to make the most of it.

Busy Beauty, the startup they had founded during their sophomore year at Babson College, had now grown to the point where they needed investment. Their line of no-water-needed personal care products was attracting attention. It included moisturizing shaving gel, dry shampoo, and body wipes, which "allow women to get ready and feel beautiful faster." They had already gotten traction through their retail and e-commerce partners, and they had new products ready for production to expand their product line. Consumers were going to love them!

They knew they were on the brink of reaching that next level if only they could get the investment needed to fund it. There was so much on the line with this meet and greet.

Sitting in the investors' conference room surrounded by steel and glass, Jamie and Michael looked around the upscale offices feeling a little intimidated. After waiting for about ten minutes, the investor hurriedly entered with a serious look and sat at the head of the table. Jamie and Michael began with some small talk, but wanted to quickly get into what was happening with Busy Beauty. As Jamie began to explain how they were building the brand, the investor held up his hand. Stop. Jamie stopped, and she and Michael exchanged a look of confusion.

"I want to see the full pitch, the real thing, how you would do it for a presentation."

They hadn't planned on this. Michael jumped up and grabbed his laptop, quickly searching for the right deck to put on the screen. He couldn't find it, and they had no handouts. Luckily they had been fundraising for a few months and knew how to pitch in all kinds of ways.

Michael found a deck that would do, and they jumped right in. No time to hook up a projector, they put the laptop in front of the investor and spoke from memory about how the pitch unfolds in the deck.

They had also nailed down from previous pitches which one of them would answer certain types of questions during Q&A. Jamie handled questions about marketing, and Michael handled operations and fundraising. The investor was impressed. Each time he threw a question their way, they were ready with a quick and complete answer. While they hadn't thought it would be this kind of meeting, their presentation and practice meant they could handle it with flying colors.

In this chapter, I am going to cover best practices for pitch preparation and presentation, but I want to begin with a word of caution. While I recommend that you prepare for and practice your pitch as much as possible, keep in mind that things aren't always going to go as planned. Things could change with little or no warning. As the Busy Beauty story illustrates, the more you prepare for your pitch, the better you are going to be able to handle whatever comes your way.

FIRST IMPRESSIONS LAST

Your pitch is your opportunity to make a positive first impression and to demonstrate that you have the chops to make a great partner and are the kind of person another entrepreneur would want to spend significant time with. It is a chance to show off your personality and emotional intelligence.

Many a potential funder has walked away from a business deal because, quite frankly, they didn't like, trust, or believe in the founder. Research shows that people make up their mind in ninety seconds or less if they want to hear more about an idea.

Entrepreneurs that convey confidence and social adaptability are more likely to be persuasive.[24] If the impression you leave through your pitch is one of an ill-prepared or flustered founder, you are dead in the water. On the other hand, if you present yourself as prepared, knowledgeable, enthusiastic, and sincere, your chances for success increase markedly.

Remember, as they get to know you through your pitch, investors and mentors are deciding if your venture is worth their time and money. They are also assessing whether you and your partners are worth their time and money. It's a cliché because it's true: *You never get a second chance to make a first impression.*

Before heading into a pitch, consider the investor's interests and motivations going into the meeting. They will certainly have an agenda in their heads as well. Spend time before your pitch considering what this might be; put yourself in their shoes. By doing some research on the people you'll be meeting with in advance, you might be able to discern what some of their concerns are, or where they'll be looking for alignment to their own industry expertise or interests.

WHAT DO I DO WITH MY HANDS?

Body language is very telling, so it's especially important to be conscious of your non-verbal communication in a pitch situation. Movement can be a window to emotions, so how you walk, stand, and gesture, even eye contact and other facial expressions, give

---

24   Manuela N. Hoehn-Weiss, Candida G. Brush, and Robert A. Baron, "Putting Your Best Foot Forward?: Assessments of Entrepreneurial Social Competence from Two Perspectives," The Journal of Private Equity 7, no. 4 (2004): 17-26.

away information about how you feel and what you are thinking. Learning to be comfortable in your own skin so you appear authentic, confident, and relaxed is one of the most important aspects of preparing to pitch.

When my students are practicing their pitches, they most frequently ask, *what do I do with my hands?* And believe or not, that is a very important question. You want your audience to focus on what you are saying without being distracted by how you are saying it.

Pay attention to how much or how little you talk with your hands. Do you flail your arms about or gesture non-stop? The last thing you want is for your hand gestures to take over as the main focus of your presentation.

I've attended pitches where the presenters had obviously over-rehearsed their hand gestures. In one instance at a TechStars Demo Day in Boston, the entrepreneur's hand gestures were big, wide, and flowing. It was the kind of over-choreographed presentation that, if you turned the sound off, you might have thought you were watching some kind of interpretive dance performance.

At the other extreme are the people who just stand still without any motion at all, arms glued to their sides. Nobody wants to watch a robot give a pitch (unless, of course, you're at an AI presentation and the robot is demonstrating cutting edge technology). A certain amount of hand gesturing is a good thing when it's done right, adding energy to your presence in the room and on the stage.

Your hand gestures should help people picture what you're talking about. For instance, let's say you're talking about a gap in some process or solution that's related to your startup. If you hold your hands up about a foot apart, in a vertical direction, palm facing palm, thumbs up, while you're emphasizing the existence of the gap, you're enhancing that image-based word, *gap*, with a gesture that's appropriate to the conversation. You're providing a symbol listeners can relate to. It works.

It's not just upper body movements that presenters need to be careful of. Some people are consumed with a lot of nervous energy when they get up in front of an audience. One way people deal with that energy is pacing. Don't do it. Don't pace.

Instead, plant yourself on stage in a spot where everyone can see you. Then it's okay to move a little, to walk to the other side of the stage and plant yourself there for a bit. But moving back and forth while you're talking is going to give your audience vertigo.

Maintaining eye contact is also important, particularly when you're pitching one-on-one. In an up-close-and-personal setting, the best practice is to look a person in the eye when you're talking. If you look down or away or fail to make eye contact at all, you lose an important opportunity to connect on a personal level; and you might even come off a bit shady, definitely not the impression you want to make.

If you are pitching in a one-to-several scenario like in a small group, be careful about who you make eye contact with and for how long. You don't want to shake anyone up with your best version of a death stare. Try to catch different people's eyes and stay with them for a good few beats while you're talking. That level of eye contact makes a huge difference because they're not going to look away. They'll stay engaged, paying more attention to you and what you're saying.

Try to be cognizant of any nervous habits you may have developed over the years. Maybe you put your hair behind your ear or move your bangs out of your face when you're talking. You may have a habit of putting your hand under your chin or pulling on your beard when you are emphasizing a point. If you find yourself engaging in these types of behaviors once or twice, that's probably fine. But if you find that you do them all the time, think about how to break these habits. While unconscious and inadvertent on your part, repetitive and quirky affectations will draw the audience focus from what you are saying to how you look saying it.

In the same vein, watch for delay behaviors, things you do to give yourself time to think. Typically, people buy time when speaking by saying "um" or "like," throwaway sounds and words that give the brain a chance to catch up with the next thought bubbling to the surface. But those "ums" and "likes" detract from what you are saying. Work on eliminating them by practicing with someone who will point out when you do these things and help you find alternative ways to take a pause. You can also use your phone to record yourself practicing your pitch to listen for these kinds of delay tactics.

Tone of voice is also important. If you're a woman, you don't want to come off too squeaky high, but you don't want to go too low either. And if you're a man, you need to be careful that you don't speak in your lowest register, the one that sounds like a cross between a grunt and a growl. Avoid ending sentences on a high note, that uptick in pitch that makes every statement sound like a question and conveys that you're unsure of yourself.

Volume and speed are also factors. I have a friend who makes a point of speaking a bit more softly in high-pressure situations. As people lean in closer to listen, they're engaging their bodies, and then their minds follow. Remember to talk slowly enough so that people can understand what you're saying but not so slowly that they're becoming frustrated or dying for you to...get...to...the...next...word already.

CHECK EMOTIONS AT THE DOOR

Be prepared to get your feelings hurt. You're putting your baby out there for the world to see, and sometimes people tell you your baby is ugly. It can be painful to hear that your pride and joy is not necessarily seen by everyone in the same light.

You might make a mistake during your pitch and embarrass yourself. It has happened to all of us. The trick, as the saying goes, is never let them see you sweat.

If somebody insults you or your business, if you say something the wrong way or are not happy with the job you did, your emotional reaction, if you are not careful, will come through in your body language. And you might not even be aware that it's happening.

Slumping over, lowering your head, and rolling your shoulders in are all signs of feeling defeated. Defensive postures might come as crossing your arms, averting your eyes from making contact, or taking a few steps backward. You need to make sure you're not letting the emotions of the moment reflect in your body language.

Entrepreneurial Negotiations, by Sam Dinnar and Lawrence

Susskind,[25] speaks to the idea that if you prepare yourself for an emotional response, you'll be better able to avoid falling victim to that response. Try coming up with a word that you can say to yourself when you recognize that your emotions might be getting the better of you, as a way to alert yourself that you need to take a breath or switch into "curious" mode. Even better, adopt some type of empowerment phrase, such as *great feedback, let's dig into that...* to help you switch gears and take what could have been an emotional trigger and convert it into an opportunity to learn. Leaning into the criticism shows that you have the humility and openness to take educated opinions seriously and gratefully, that you are an active and interested listener, and as we've discussed before, coachable.

You know the ins and outs of your value proposition, you have created a solid 4H Framework flow for your pitch, and you've created a kick-ass deck to communicate it.

Now it's time to dot those i's and cross those t's.

PRACTICAL CONSIDERATIONS BEFORE THE BIG DAY

If you are familiar with Murphy's Law, you already know that anything that can go wrong will go wrong. The trick is having a Plan B so you are ready to compensate if (when?) Plan A goes awry.

The following, while not exhaustive, is a list of matters to address prior to your big day:

---

25 Sam Dinnar and Lawrence Susskind, *Entrepreneurial Negotiation: Understanding and Managing the Relationships that Determine Your Entrepreneurial Success,* Palgrave Macmillan; 1st ed. 2019 edition (August 17, 2018), 61.

- **Dress for success.** Choose clothing that is professional without being stiff. Usually business casual is the way to go, but that doesn't mean you shouldn't strive to be yourself. If you like to rock a three-piece suit, then go for it. If you have multiple piercings or sport an armful of ink, feel free to show off that bling and those tats. Think tasteful authenticity, clean and neat, and you can't go wrong. And just to be on the safe side, bring along an extra shirt or skirt in case you do get a coffee spill on that carefully selected ensemble.

- **Recon the room.** Know the audio-visual lay of the land and plan your equipment needs accordingly. Bring back-up power cords and clickers, in case the ones you were promised aren't there on pitch day, and don't forget that dongle you are going to need to hook up your laptop to your host venue's projector. Also have a stick drive in your bag in case you need to move your deck file to another computer. Bring actual paper copies of your deck in case the power goes out and you have to wing the presentation old-school. (But don't hand out paper copies of your deck before your talk unless you have to, the audience will be too tempted to look ahead.)

- **Thoroughly research your attendees ahead of time.** Know how many people will be in attendance, and if possible, find out their names. Learn about their backgrounds, interests, and preferences to the extent possible. You should know if they've ever invested in your industry before, if they've invested in a competitor or potential competitor. Are they an expert in the industry? What connections might they have that you would like to meet? This will not only prove beneficial as you put the finishing touches on your deck, but knowing who you are speaking to and what floats their boats is useful when prepping for Q&A. We'll talk more about audiences in Part 2 of this book.

- **Determine the role of each presenter.** If you have co-founders or other members of the team in attendance, you should decide in advance who is going to present which part of the pitch and who will answer what in the Q&A. If you do split it up, make sure that each person can nail their own part but also is conversant enough in the entire presentation to pinch hit if necessary. Remembering Murphy's Law, you need to be able to jump in if your partner comes down with laryngitis or some other affliction on pitch day.

- **Stay in character.** Last year, I was in a pitch session where the two co-founders decided to tag team the presentation. The problem began when, as soon as co-founder number one finished with his portion of the pitch and sat down, he picked up his phone and started checking his messages while his partner was presenting. His lack of engagement and rudeness to both his co-founder and his audience did not endear him to any would-be funders. Remember that you are going to be in the hot seat, even when you're sitting down. Stay in your role and in character.

- **Practice Q&A, then practice Q&A more.** Even if you are usually great on your feet, Q&A *may* be jarring and difficult. And if you're not used to being good on your feet, Q&A *will* be jarring and difficult. Make sure you practice Q&A ahead of time with someone who isn't on your team, who may not know a ton about your business, and who can ask hard questions.

- **Be prepared to address risks.** Early-stage investing is inherently risky, so theoretically investors in early-stage startups expect higher rewards. But a topic on their mind as they listen to you is what are the risks with this business, what could go wrong? Be prepared to address any areas where pieces of your plan have significant risk. Be honest and transparent about these things and show a thoughtful answer regarding your Plan B. For example, if you are relying on a factory in China for a particular part and the commercial reality is that the President is threatening higher tariffs on Chinese goods, be up front about the risk, and let your investors know that you have considered contingencies and supply chain workarounds. Include a slide about this in your appendix, and be prepared to toggle over to it if needed.

- **Know your numbers.** Sometimes an investor will want you to address a certain key metric such as customer acquisition costs to help them assess the future profitability of their investment. You will lose all credibility if you don't know things like unit economics and customer acquisition costs cold. While you don't need to present detailed financial statements in your first pitch, make sure you can address any big assumptions that went into the business model like margins or selling costs. Be prepared to discuss the details of your marketing strategies, like whether to go with Facebook ads, how to boost Google SEO organically, or why using influencers to market your product or service makes sense and how that will pay out for you. Much of the detail on these things will be projections at this point in your journey, but if you can give thoughtful answers to these kinds of questions, investors and mentors will have further validation of your smarts.

- **Understand and address the competition.** Do you know who your top competitors are and what distinguishes your company from the leader in the field? Be ready to identify the competition and explain why and how you can penetrate an established industry or break off into a new market. I've seen pitches where the entrepreneur will say there is no competition in the space they are planning to go into. This is a huge mistake. Experienced businesspeople know that there is always competition even if it's not a direct competitor. There could be substitutes that offer the same ultimate benefit or an indirect competitor who hasn't yet gone into this exact space but has the ability to eventually go there.

- **Be prepared for the out-of-pocket costs of pitching.** Establish a pitching budget and make sure you're not caught short if the investor of your dreams finally summons you to her offices. Pitching costs for things like travel and slide deck copies can add up; and you could end up with unusual and unanticipated expenses along the way. My friend Dan, the founder of an ice cream company, realized that every time he had to demo his product, which meant at every pitch, he needed to transport ice cream in dry ice to the tune of two hundred bucks per trip.

- **Be more than prepared to go off the presentation—be delighted if this happens to you!** If you're presenting to a single person or a small group and they start to ask questions about some area of your pitch, don't be thrown off your game if you never get through your entire deck. In fact, be prepared to go completely off deck and wing it. As long as you've prepared, you can embrace the opportunity to connect with your audience and dig deeper into the aspects of your business that interests them the most. Seize the opportunity to convert a pitch into a fruitful conversation.

- **Be energetic and avoid jargon.** Let your geek flag fly! You are an expert in every way about your industry; you know things that others don't. Enthusiasm and deep knowledge will work in your favor. Be careful, however, that you don't let your enthusiasm make you forget that your goal is to communicate your story and your vision. Toward that end, be mindful of your use of insider jargon, acronyms, or technical words that your audience won't understand.

ENTREPRENEUR ETIQUETTE

The entrepreneurship game is very relationship-based. How you treat people matters in every interaction. If you get a reputation as someone who doesn't follow up or is flaky or unkind when you think no one is looking, word will travel fast and you'll soon find yourself out of the game. Be aware that your reputation will both precede and follow you. Back-channeling techniques, when an investor or mentor seeks out people who know you or have worked with you and asks pointed questions about the "real you," are common in the startup world. You need to garner a reputation as a trustworthy person who is a decent human being, regardless of scene or circumstance.

Consider the people you meet at the front desk of the offices and venues you will visit. These folks are the gatekeepers to every-thing, so make the extra effort to get to know them. Don't go off on the receptionist because you can't get your parking validated. If you do, you can be sure that the partner or investor will hear about it. Be your most professional, polite, personable self because everyone you meet matters.

After the pitch, thank everyone in the room. Try to get business cards so you can follow up with each person individually. Send a personal note to the people who gave up their time to attend your pitch, and thank them for doing so. Feel free to emphasize certain points that you think are important, but focus more on any direct feedback they gave you or any comments they made. If they asked a question that you couldn't answer on the spot, the post-meeting email is a good time to provide your response. Anytime you have a legitimate reason to reach out to someone personally, for example if you followed some advice they gave you and want to report on the good results, go ahead and send a personal note. Email is fine for a thank-you note, but if you really want to impress someone, try going full-out, old-school and sending a handwritten note of thanks.

BEST PRACTICE: THE QUARTERLY EMAIL UPDATE

After each and every pitch, you are going to get lists of attendees and business cards. Be sure to add these people to your email database. In doing so, you are building an important asset for your company, an email list of people who are already interested in what you are doing, whether or not they invested or became an advisor.

I counsel the entrepreneurs I work with to create a quarterly email for this list of people, updating them on what's happened over the last quarter. Updates can include things like sharing any successes you've had in reaching your investment or business goals, as well as any lessons you have learned. You can also share problems you are looking to solve and questions you need help with in the upcoming quarter, followed by an ask for help. The asks for help can be simple things like inquiring if anyone has a connection in your industry they can provide or a referral for a good lawyer. Or maybe you have some burning issue you need help with and want to know if anyone in this group of allies might have experiences or advice to share.

People love to help when they know exactly what you need. And odds are they'll be happy to hear from you once a quarter to know how things are going. This keeps these relationships warm, and you never know when someone might be impressed enough to jump back in to invest.

Here is an example of a quarterly update email:

To: StartupCo Advisors
From: Sereta Nious
Date: April 1, 2019
Subject: StartupCo Update for Advisors and Investors

Things have been busy at StartupCo, we're making a ton of great progress. Here are the details.

Accomplishments for Q2
Product Improvement: Our beta testing told us that we needed to improve our internal messaging system. The tech

team went to work and in record time has released version one to the platform for customer feedback. Let us know if you have a chance to try this.

New Team Members: We are excited to welcome two new team members—Lucy will join us in an operations role and Brett is leading our business development efforts with enterprise clients. Check them out on LinkedIn.

Pitch Win! We were excited to win the New Venture Challenge last week. In addition to the $10K first prize, we met some incredible people who have already made important introductions for us. Thanks to Casey P. for all her follow-up from the event.

KPIs: We hit our target KPIs for the quarter. New Clients: 4; Renewal Rate: 85%.

Key Learnings
Pricing Model: We're moving away from the freemium model we started with. We've had good success in getting some new beta clients to pay so we are anxious to work on this further.

Next Steps
Product: We'll be fine-tuning our algorithm based on this last round of data we have from our beta clients. We think this will allow for stronger results out of the matching process.

Business Development: We'll be at AI Expo at the end of

this month. We have several big client meetings planned, and have secured a spot on the demo stage during Day 2. Looking forward to making the most of this opportunity.

Asks

Connections: Do you have any connections in the financial services industry? We are looking to meet heads of marketing. Please let us know and we can provide copy for intro emails to make it easy to introduce us.

Talent: We're still looking to find a backend architect for the product team. If you have any ideas please let us know. The job description is <u>here</u>.

Any comments or questions on this update are welcome! Please keep the feedback flowing, we love to hear from you. Thank you, as always, for your incredible support.

The StartupCo Team
SeretaN@startupco.com

Finally, a word about social media. Do not celebrate—or complain!—on social media about your meeting. Do Not Do It.

Some people prefer to keep these meetings private and don't want the world to know about their schedule or connections. This is the case even if the meeting was perfect. If something went wrong, the last place you want to air your dirty laundry or dis a potential investor or mentor is in a public online forum. Rest assured, every person who even considers investing or working with you is going to back-channel on you. Everyone does it. And that is going to include checking out your social media.

Make sure that all of your social media reflects the kind of person you want your investor to see. The people who work with early-stage entrepreneurs do it because they love the people and the process. Be the person that you would invest in if the roles were reversed.

TAKE ACTION: UNDERSTAND WHAT YOUR BODY LANGUAGE IS SAYING

The best way to improve your body language is to find ways to observe yourself, note areas for improvement, and then keep practicing until you are confident your body language is sending the right message to your audience. Try these techniques:

- Do a full uninterrupted run-through of your pitch in an office or conference room that's as close to the real environment as possible.
- Have a friend or colleague use your phone or a video camera to record your pitch.
- Go through the recording a few times both with the sound on and the sound off and see if you notice places where you are falling into some of the body language traps or vocal practices that send the wrong signals.
- Ask a friend to watch your pitch recording and look for gestures and other non-verbal movements that distract from the presentation or send negative signals. Then have them listen to the recording without watching, again for

the purpose of finding tone of voice issues that negatively impact your presentation. Listen to their feedback and try the pitch again, eliminating the behaviors.

- Do it again, then watch it again.
- Keep practicing until you can run through your entire pitch keeping your body language, tone of voice, and gesturing on target.

PART II

Know Your Audience

CHAPTER 9

Understanding Audiences

Twin brothers Michael and Matthew Vega-Sanz sat in their Babson College dorm room in 2017 craving their favorite pizza and bemoaning the fact that not only did the pizza place not deliver, but they didn't have a car.

The nearby student parking lot was full of cars that were just sitting there, cars that would be oh-so-useful as transportation for running out for, say, a couple of large-sized pepperoni pizzas. If only there were some way students could access cars for short errands like pizza runs. Then the idea struck them: why not create a peer-to-peer car-sharing service targeting the college student market?

Just like that, Lula, the first car-sharing platform in the country that offers rentals to college students as young as eighteen, was conceived.

Michael and Matthew decided to pitch Lula at a regional competition hosted by student-centric personal finance company SoFi and won. SoFi flew them out to their headquarters in San Francisco for dinner and discussions with their executives.

At dinner, the twins strategically chose to sit near SoFi co-founder Dan Macklin, hoping to start a relationship with him. It worked! After this first meeting, they bombarded Dan with online messages, updating him on Lula, asking him questions about startups, and bringing up other topics that they thought might grab his attention. Sometimes Dan answered, other times he did not.

More than six months later, Dan reached out to the young entrepreneurs via LinkedIn. He mentioned that he was leaving SoFi and looking at becoming an advisor for a few early-stage companies. He wanted to know if Lula would like to talk.

Matthew and Michael knew it would boost Lula's reputation and value if an established entrepreneur like Dan not only wanted to work with them, but believed in their company enough to actually join them as an investor.

Michael flew to San Francisco to meet face-to-face with Dan, who agreed to join him for an early breakfast at a downtown café. Assuming Dan would want to spend most of the time discussing the business, Michael had taken great pains to make sure he was prepared to discuss any aspect of Lula that

Dan showed interest in. To his surprise, Dan started asking him personal questions.

"He wanted to learn about me, my family, my motivations, my desires, and my passions," Michael explains. "He wanted to know who I was as a person, all about who he was investing in. We shared stories about family, hardships, and joyous moments in our lives. And then, toward the end of the breakfast, we finally discussed the business."

Dan asked about the founders' vision for the company, their go-to-market strategy, and how they would position themselves to beat the competition. Michael's pitch was ready with the answers to all these questions. Completely at ease with Dan, Michael was able to tell Lula's story in a compelling way, modifying it on the fly to show specifically how Dan could be helpful and where his expertise would be most needed. As the meeting came to an end, Dan was excited, and Michael knew the chemistry was just right. Dan decided to invest in Lula, a move that would add rocket fuel to the startup.

In Part I of this book, I covered brand marketing tools like storytelling and positioning statements that entrepreneurs can adopt to help their startups attract investors and mentors. I'd like to add to the mix another lesson from the classical marketing world: the competitive advantage that comes from understanding what makes your target audience tick.

In the context of brand marketing, the audience is your customer. In the context of early-stage startup pitching, the audience is whomever you approach for money, mentorship, or more. As Lula founders Michael and Matthew learned, pitching is personal, and building relationships is every bit as important as demonstrating business smarts.

In this chapter, I will cover some of the things you should learn about various types of pitch audiences, how venue impacts a pitch, and how gaining insight into audience motivations and experiences can turn a good pitch into a great pitch. Then, in chapter 10, I will show you several different sources of potential funding, a few you have probably considered and a few you might not yet have thought of.

FOUNDER: KNOW THY INVESTOR

If your goal is to knock your pitch out of the park, you must take the time to investigate each specific audience that you will be pitching. You want to walk into the pitch with enough knowledge to speak *to them*, rather than just giving a canned pitch aimed *at them*.

The kind of knowledge I am referring to goes beyond what you find on their public LinkedIn profile, like what they do and where they've worked. I am talking about finding connections on a personal level.

Find out where they went to school. There may be a connection you can make based on their alma mater or on yours. Find out about their hobbies and interests. Did they play a sport in college? Are they a tennis fanatic now? Are they a wine lover or do they have a passion for pizza? Do they volunteer with or serve on the board of any nonprofits?

Did you both grow up on the streets of the inner city? Or attend a prep school in the suburbs? Do you hail from a region of the country that gives you a similar world view or subtext you can bond over? If you've ever sat in a meeting with two people from Texas, you'll know exactly what I mean. People from the Lone Star State just seem to get along.

School connections, hobbies, and outside-of-work passions are all commonalities that can be powerful. It's uncanny what you can find out about people once you start digging. Social media is a great source for finding a point where you and someone you are pitching to can connect as humans.

You might not always find detailed information about every person you pitch to, but you should devote some time to investigating the backgrounds, preferences, and investing histories of the relevant people in your audience. At the very least, you should have gathered enough intelligence to be able to intuit which pitch points warrant emphasis and which can be skimmed over. Try to find the answers to questions such as:

- Have they ever invested or worked in your industry? (If so, what was the outcome?)
- Have they invested in or are they considering investing in a competitor?
- How good is their network in this space?
- How much involvement do they expect to have in the company on a daily or monthly basis?
- Do they invest in follow-up rounds?
- Do they ever lead investment rounds?
- What is their typical check size?

- How many investments per year do they do and where are they in their annual cycle?
- What's the status of their current fund?
- What kind of help, besides money, do they provide to founders?

Sarah Hodges, an early-stage VC and former founder, emphasizes the importance of knowing your audience by putting it this way:

> Research the investor you're pitching in advance and tailor your materials accordingly. This is an important step to ensure that they're a potential fit for your business, but the exercise will also help you make sure you're presenting the right information. If they're data-driven, include numbers that describe why your business is compelling. If they've shown a history of investing in similar business models, make sure you know this. If they've voiced a particular concern about your industry, get in front of it in your messaging.

As I said earlier, investors see thousands of pitches each year and end up funding only a small percentage of them. The goal here is to stand out from the crowd. That is what will give you a competitive advantage.

VARIABLES ABOUT YOUR AUDIENCE TO CONSIDER

Along with intelligence-gathering on specific people you are pitching, I have isolated a few key variables about the environment and audience to take into account as you prepare each pitch.

AUDIENCE SIZE AND VENUE

The number of people you have before you and the location will make a big impact on how you pitch.

If you are going to be pitching in a large auditorium-style setting, you will need to put on a show. In this scenario, you will likely stick with a pre-planned and highly produced presentation. The audience will expect a formal, tight, well-rehearsed performance. While they want to see what's new and next, they also want to be entertained. If you want to hold their attention, you are going to have to do your best to balance being informative and projecting magnetic energy that fills the room.

Remember that when you are putting on a show, all eyes are on you. The communication is going to be one way with you as presenter and audience as receiver, at least until you get to the Q&A part, if there is one.

When meeting with a few investors in a small group, for example in an angel group screening meeting, the surroundings might feel a bit more intimate, but remember that there are several people present and you need to keep them all engaged. If this is a pregame for the actual pitch, this audience is going to be gauging whether or not you deserve a stab at their bigger membership. If that is the case, keep your showman's hat on.

If you are pitching one-on-one, sitting across the table from an investor, your interaction will generally move to more of a conversation-like experience. Ideally, there will be a friendly tone to it. But that doesn't mean you should be less prepared or forego creating a stellar pitch deck. Even if you don't use it at the meeting, you should have it ready to use opportunistically. You may want to reference a particular slide or chart in the deck to help clarify a point in the conversation.

Believe it or not, some of the most productive and fruitful one-on-one meetings between founders and investors happen in the most informal settings of all: coffee shops. In fact, it's not unusual for founders to set up several back-to-back investor meetings over coffee in a single day. Scenarios like these are so prevalent in the startup world that I thought about calling this chapter, "I'm over-caffeinated and sweaty," as a sort of homage to all the early-stage entrepreneurs I know who have become "let's get coffee" regulars. While this venue is informal versus the "show," keep your focus on giving a professional pitch; it can be distracting to be in a busy, public spot for both you and your listener. Watch your potential investor's interest in your conversation and be prepared to adjust if his body language or comments suggest he isn't entirely engaged.

ABILITY TO CONNECT ON A PERSONAL LEVEL

A successful pitch connects on a personal level with the audience. In larger venues, this idea comes into play by trying to hook the audience emotionally so that as a group they start to feel invested in you and cheering for your success. You can accomplish this by storytelling and showing your personality through how you present. With this situation, however, you are not creating an individual connection.

In smaller group situations or one-on-one meetings, connecting on a personal level during the pitch can have big impact. You can sense this when the pitch moves from being a presentation to being a conversation. Your business smarts shine of course, but also investors can see more about you, learn about your backstory and what you value. It's an opportunity for both of you to see if there is good working chemistry to build on. Here, you need to be good on your feet and more flexible in the moment to shift from business to personal and back again. Like the breakfast meeting between Michael and Dan in the Lula story, the interaction could turn up-close-and-personal for a while, but at the end of the day business will always be discussed. Knowing beforehand that there is a possibility to get more personal will help you prepare.

INVESTOR SOPHISTICATION

Are you pitching to professional investors like angels or seed VCs, or are you pitching to people with varied backgrounds who may or may not have much experience with early-stage startups? Sometimes pitch competition judges might be event sponsors or key executives who are not professional investors but do have some business knowledge.

Professional investors will be looking more critically at what you say and do from an investment perspective, whereas judges in a pitch competition, who may or may not be intimately familiar and experienced with investing in early-stage companies, may also look at other factors. Depending on the objective of the event, judges might take into account factors such as how much momentum you have experienced as you got your startup running, the social impact you might have, or just the quality of your pitch presentation.

FIELDING AUDIENCE QUESTIONS OR FEEDBACK

In some pitch situations you will be expected to answer questions and/or receive feedback from judges, potential investors, or the audience. This can come during your pitch, but most often it is saved for a section at the very end. Ideally you will have anticipated common questions about your pitch and have prepared to answer them in a tight, complete way. You can't ramble on in these situations, you need to be concise.

You might also get a question you can't or don't want to answer. If it's a "can't answer" question, I would be honest and say that. But offer to follow up with the answer afterward once you've had time to find it or research it; say something like *"That's a great question, but unfortunately I don't have the answer for it at this moment. I'd like to get back to you after this with a complete answer, does that work?"*

A "don't want to answer" question is harder. If it's because you are in front of a large audience, I'd respond, *"That's something that requires some detail to answer, probably better to cover it offline with you afterward."* A skilled presenter who is good on his feet could answer with something related, or reframe the question to something more in-bounds, but not directly answer the off-limits question. With practice, you can get good at this.

As we covered in previous chapters, it's crucial that you remember not to get defensive (verbally or non-verbally) in the Q&A session if someone provides feedback that is negative. Demonstrate your coachability, and graciously accept the feedback.

GETTING FAMILIAR

One last note to consider as you prepare for each pitch is the extent of your personal relationships with anyone in your audience. How familiar are they to you? Is there anyone in the audience you have previously met either socially or in a business context?

If you share a closeness or past history with your prospective investor, this might compel you to cross over to a level of informality that could actually damage your credibility. Look to the investor to dictate the level of formality, and never let familiarity impact your level of politeness or consideration. Regardless of the audience, acquaintance or friend or stranger, you need to keep it professional, even if the meeting turns somewhat less formal.

Whether running from coffee shop to coffee shop to pitch one-on-one, or standing on a stage in front of hundreds, or some type of presentation scenario in between, the key to success is preparation and practice. The goal is to highlight the most important aspects of your venture while engaging your audience.

Now that you've gotten a handle on different pitch environments, let's look at some different sources of funding for your startup and examine their perspective on your pitch.

CHAPTER 10

Pitching for Money: Early-Stage Funding Sources

WAKU'S EARLY FUNDING JOURNEY

Juan Giraldo and Nico Estrella had no delusions about what it was going to take to fund Waku, their startup consumer brand that offered a unique, plant-based, Ecuadorian, wellness tea. If they were going to take advantage of the public's penchant for trendy, plant-based, health foods, time was of the essence. They needed to raise money fast.

Many entrepreneurs start with family, but that wasn't an option for Juan. He had borrowed from family members for an earlier venture that produced no return, so he knew the family well was dry, at least until he could prove some traction with Waku.

Juan approached some close friends, people who knew him

and believed in him and in what he and Nico were doing. After pitching Waku in a series of one-on-one conversations, he was able to raise $50,000, enough to keep the company moving ahead.

"When you look at our fundraising history, a lot of people would never even have started," Juan said. "We just kept moving forward. We had only $50K in the bank to do what would probably take $500K. But we were confident we just needed to hit a milestone to get more people excited and find more capital. You just gotta go."

Emphasizing Waku's Ecuadorian origin story, which clearly resonated with the public, Juan and Nico developed a very successful crowdfunding campaign, allowing them to fund their forays into test markets while developing new flavors for their product line. Next, they applied for and received a grant from the country of Ecuador.

After this, and more traction with the business, Juan pursued angel funding. Since he had launched the company from Boston, he focused on angels in the New England area who had credibility in his industry. He knew that getting even one of these angels on board would not only help get other angels to follow, but also bring valuable expertise to the company. Finding the right angels, Juan explains, took time.

"On average, it took us six to twelve months to receive investment from angels," he says. "We convinced them to join us by delivering on what we said we were going to deliver, and by showing traction and results over time. They were focused on making sure the business fundamentals were strong and having evidence that we could be successful together."

Juan and Nico also approached their suppliers and manufacturing partners for better terms that would relieve cash flow pressures. They shared their growth strategy and forecasts of the volume the company would need in order to meet manufacturing projections over the next three years. Juan painted a picture for the suppliers of how much he would buy if Waku were successful and how the vendor would benefit from the company's growth. Juan and Nico banked on the fact that these suppliers, with whom they had built relationships of trust over the course of eighteen months, would jump at the chance to work with a business that could help them penetrate the coveted U.S. market. The suppliers came on board providing better terms on the accounts payable, freeing up cash to run the business.

Waku continued to hustle to raise money during the early stages of the company, eventually turning to an angel network and a bank loan as they got more established.

Juan's advice for other entrepreneurs? "You are always fundraising; so keep your pitch deck and forecasts updated, and have the documents ready to sign if the investor is excited to go forward."

As Waku's funding story shows, depending on what stage you are in your entrepreneurial journey, there are many places to find money and mentors to help.

The following page sets forth some familiar and perhaps not-so-familiar sources to target in the early stage of fundraising for your startup. I also provide a high-level sense of how the four variables from the previous chapter play out when pitching these investors.

FRIENDS AND FAMILY FUNDING

Friends, family members, and others in your personal network might be the first people you think of approaching for funding. For most startup entrepreneurs, friends and family won't be sophisticated investors and probably won't have the expertise to help you from a process standpoint. They are helping you because they are the people who know you best, they believe in you, and they want to be part of your success story.

While approaching friends and family for investment is a good place to start, it can also be tricky. You are asking the people closest to you to take a very big risk. I always advise that you should be clear with your friends or family about *all* the potential risks involved in investing in an early-stage startup. The harsh reality is that there is a high likelihood that they won't get their money back, so make sure they understand this and are able to afford a loss.

I also think it's important to have professional documentation of expectations around this kind of investment. Lay out the expectations of how you will interact on both sides of the deal so when things get sticky, as they always do on the road to startup success, you have a guide for how everyone should behave. You may think it would be nice to have your brother-in-law as an investor, but how will he be when times are tough? You don't want to be in

Sources of Early Stage Funds and Variables to Consider About Your Audience

Large Audience: There will be little to no interaction with the audience; communication is mostly one way. Generally, these environments are more like a "show" or performance where it is hard to pivot your presentation in response to what's happening in the moment.

Personal Connection: This is more of a meeting where the pitch is mixed with an opportunity for the investor to get to know your personality and test for personal chemistry.

High Investor Sophistication: In these scenarios you are pitching to professional investors who have invested in early stage startups many times. This audience will be more focused on metrics, trends, and numbers than one consisting of mostly general business people.

Audience Questions/Feedback: You can expect to answer questions and receive feedback in the moment, either during your pitch or at the end, in a formal (not conversational) way. Be prepared to be quick on your feet and to demonstrate coachability and active listening.

Sources of Early Stage Funds	Large Audience	Personal Connection	High Investor Sophistication	Audience Questions/ Feedback
Friends and Family		✔		
Angel Investor		✔	✔	✔
Angel Groups	✔		✔	✔
Seed Stage VC		✔	✔	✔
Startup Accelerator Demo Day	✔		✔	
Open Pitch Competition	✔			✔
Family Office		✔	✔	✔
Vendors		✔		
Banks			✔	
Government-backed Loans			✔	
Non-Profit Grants				
Strategic Investors		✔		
Crowdfunding	✔			

a position where family ties could be forever broken by a deal gone wrong.

These pitches are usually one-on-one or one-on-two, with opportunity to adjust and flex as needed to put yourself in the best light.

ANGEL INVESTORS

Individual angel investors are people who use their own money to invest in startups. This type of investor can be distinguished from angel investor groups and a venture capitalist (both discussed later). To an angel, the investment is personal.

Often the angel wants to roll up his or her sleeves and get down and dirty with the business. It's pretty rare for a VC to back an early startup until it has some traction or evidence of product-market fit, while angels love the opportunities, challenges, and adrenaline rushes that come from working with a new venture from the ground up.

Angels are often entrepreneurs themselves or people who have otherwise been very successful in the business world. Usually, they have a particular expertise in or affinity for a certain industry and seek opportunities to invest in early-stage ventures. These are folks who love having skin in the game, who live for helping to bring early-stage ideas to life. An angel is certainly after an eventual, and hopefully handsome, return on their investment, there is no doubt about that; but they are equally or even more motivated by the process. They get a real charge out of being involved and working with awesome founders.

From a founder's perspective, reeling in a good, solid, angel investor has benefits beyond measure. Not only do they have money to spend, their experience and network alone are extremely valuable.

Angel investors will offer funding in return for a piece of the venture. Some may want equity in the company or they may prefer a convertible debt arrangement where they will loan the startup money that will, over time, convert to equity. In some instances, an angel may negotiate a combination of the two.

While not a hard and fast rule, it has been my general experience that angels prefer to invest in companies that are geographically close to them. While a VC in Boston or New York City might not mind investing in a company on the West Coast, angels seem to favor funding companies that are in their general area so they can be hands-on.

The initial meeting with an angel is usually one of those one-on-one encounters in a coffee shop or other "neutral" spot where you can get to know each other. Odds are you have already sent the angel your executive summary or short pitch deck in advance, so they know a little about your business before this first meeting. This is precisely the type of meeting where you don't want to achieve a level of familiarity before it's appropriate, as discussed in the last section. You'll likely start with a form of your pitch, but if it's going well, it should quickly move to two-way discussion. A good skill for entrepreneurs to learn is the ability to respond in the moment to how you think you are coming across to the angel investor and then adjust. Does it seem like you've come on too strong at first because he is leaning away from you? Slow down, take a breath, and back off a bit. Or does he seem not entirely engaged in the conversation? Shift gears with an important statistic that might be interesting to him or move to another part of your pitch.

It's actually pretty easy to find lists of angel investors and information about what they like to invest in. You can search the internet for curated lists that other people have put together as part of their own fundraising process. There are some generous and helpful founders who make their lists of angels, seed investors, or micro-seed investors available to everyone. You can also find information on angel investors on the Angel Capital Association (www.angelcapitalassociation.org) website. Another good place to look is online. There are platforms that make it easy for angel investors and founders to meet such as Angelist and Gust.

So, then what? More research. Once you think you've found someone who might be a good fit for you and your startup, do as much research on them as possible. Ideally, during this research you'll find some connection to this angel, either through someone, or someone twice removed, who knows them. This could be sharing a common educational background, former employers, nonprofit work, or even the town they live in.

Many entrepreneurs think it's hard to get to meet these people, but with a little work you can usually find some way to get a warm introduction to them or attend an event where they might show up. Check out their social media to see what events they go to or where they might be speaking. If you think about it, angels are dying to jump on board the next big thing, so they aren't hiding. And that's the key to all of this, putting in the research to find the connection to get a warm introduction.

ANGEL GROUPS

An angel group is a set of angel investors who have come together either to invest with each other as a group or to share the work of vetting interesting startups before determining if they want to invest as individuals. Regardless of whether they go in with other angels or invest alone, each angel is, at the end of the day, putting up his or her own funds.

Perhaps the big difference between pitching an angel network and an individual angel is the time it will take to get a deal. Expect to do a lot of hurrying up and waiting. When dealing with angel groups, patience is a virtue.

Typically, angel groups employ a prescreening process that includes a preliminary assessment of the business by analysts who work for the angel network. They are looking for some top-line criteria to see if the venture fits the investment preferences of the group. Sometimes they have a sector preference such as biotech, software platforms, or consumer products. They're looking to see if the business you would be pitching is in a growth area in their sector, and they want to understand where your business falls on the development spectrum. Their experts determine how much funding is needed, and then they determine whether your business meets certain parameters they may have set up for funding. The angel group wants to be sure that investors will own enough equity in a company to justify the money, time, and effort they would contribute to the enterprise.

If you make it through prescreening, you go to screening, where the members of the network take a closer look. At this stage, the members get together to review your pitch deck and determine whether there is enough interest to move you and your business forward in the process. You might even be asked to present a formal preliminary pitch to a subset of the group who are tasked with determining whether you rate an opportunity to present your pitch to the entire group at their next scheduled meeting. This is usually a formal pitch to a small group with a little flexibility to adjust based on the impression you are making on them.

When it comes time to actually pitch to the larger group (up to fifty people) in a formal setting like a board room or a classroom, keep in mind the adage I've mentioned now more than a couple of times: pitching is personal. Even though it looks like you are dealing with a group that follows rather rigid rules, when it comes down to the wire of whether or not your company will be chosen, that decision is still going to be based on who you are as much as what you are doing.

Angel investor group decisions are extremely subjective. Once you are in front of the group, the angels are going to look at factors like your work ethic, how much passion you exhibit for your business, and how transparent they think you have been. You may have the best idea in the world, but if you can't demonstrate that you have the drive and ability to execute on your vision, you are not going to make it through.

Here is why I mentioned patience at the beginning of this section on angel investor groups: even if you pass all these hurdles with flying colors and the group consensus is to fund your startup, there is still a due diligence process to go through, the results of which can sour the whole deal. During due diligence, the angels will determine how much they would be willing to invest and under what terms. It can take a long time to get an answer because they have a very defined process and are working with a lot of people at one time. Even if you pass due diligence muster, it still takes an average of four months to get funding.

Since pitching to an angel group takes up a lot of everyone's time, entrepreneurs should thoroughly research the group before going in to make sure they're a good fit. If you go the angel network route, get to know the profile of the network group and its members. Who else have they invested in? What's their track record of actually following through with funding for the startups that pitch them?

When dealing with an angel group, you definitely want to know before you go.

REACHING OUT TO POTENTIAL INVESTORS: EMAIL BEST PRACTICES

To make strong connections with potential partners, you need to develop an email outreach strategy that is polished and professional. When you find a promising connection to an angel or other investor, send them an email that pitches your startup. Use your elevator pitch here, and that includes your "ask," which in this context is the specific reason you are emailing them. If you are looking for feedback, be specific. For example, you might say, *I am looking for feedback on my website*, or *I am hoping you could provide feedback on my MVP*.

Ideally, you will say something that shows you've done your

research and know where they can add value to your company, something like, *I think your perspective on customer acquisition in SaaS tech would be helpful to me based on your past experience with HubSpot.* At the same time, be sure to include a mention of the connection you have to each other so your email doesn't end up in the spam folder.

You will need a customized subject line that will get their attention and entice them to open your email. I often recommend using the recipient's first name in the subject line and also referring to something that you know about their interests so that they know it's not totally random. For example, your subject line might say, *Bob, my AI startup, referred by Christie G.*

Another way to do this is to write an email to the person who has agreed to refer you, introducing your company and the specific "ask," and have them forward it to your prospect. The referring person can then write just a couple of sentences about how they know you and what they think about your business. If the prospect agrees to connect with you, then the referring person can just add you to the email chain, asking you to follow up on the introduction, and then get out of the way.

Ultimately getting that warm introduction is the key to the process, then you'll have the opportunity to unleash your stellar pitch.

SEED STAGE VENTURE CAPITAL

For a venture capitalist, the numbers game they play with their funds requires that they look for a return of ten times or more on their money overall. They make multiple bets knowing that most won't return at that level, but they'll have a few that so outpace the market that it will make those other losses palatable. This also means that you need to be building the type of company that has potential for exponential growth or it doesn't make sense for the VC's fund economics. VC money is pooled from investors called limited partners or LPs. The LPs that pool their money into VC funds might be individual deep-pocketed investors, or they could be large institutions. Seed-stage VCs specifically invest at the earliest stages and are skilled at identifying and developing founders.

Pitching a seed-stage VC is similar to pitching an angel in the sense that there's a lot of relationship building that goes on in the early meetings. These investors are very sophisticated and often have deep technical knowledge about the industries they invest in. At some point in the process, you will give a formal pitch as they consider whether or not to invest. This could be to the main partner you've been working with, or to a subset of the group who can advocate for you to the larger group. Expect back and forth dialogue as questions fly fast and furious. Be ready to provide detail about your assumptions and plans to de-risk the investment through experiments as you explain the business.

STARTUP ACCELERATORS

Accelerators are an effective way to get your startup off and running. You might also have heard them called incubators. The terms are often used interchangeably, but they have some key differences, mostly around duration and stage. Incubators usually support startups in the idea stage that are looking for a business model and market, with no set time period. Accelerators most often have a set duration and work with investable early-stage startups to build upon their foundations and "accelerate" them forward with intensive mentorship and investment.

In brief, an accelerator is a cohort program that begins with a pretty extensive application process. If your startup is accepted, a real feather in your cap as most accelerators are extremely competitive, you basically end up in a one-stop-shop that offers you connections, mentorship, programming, and workshops. All of this nurturing and coaching culminates in a showcase or demo day opportunity, where you get to pitch your startup to a group of interested investors.

Accelerators usually operate under a fixed-time scenario typically three to four months long, and you exchange somewhere around six percent of equity in your company for the privilege of participating. Sometimes it also comes with some cash investment that is factored into the experience you will get and the equity you are giving up. Being equity owners adds to the accelerator's incentive to see you succeed, so it can be a very good thing.

The greatest benefit you get from the better-known and prestigious accelerators such as Y Combinator, 500 Startups, or Techstars, to name a few, is the network that they connect you to. More than anything else, having access to this network of mentors and investors makes accelerators a desirable option.

Accelerators typically focus on a particular segment. For example,

I am a mentor for a Techstar accelerator program called Techstar Sports, which focuses exclusively on tech companies that are building ventures related to sports, such as fan engagement, smart stadiums, wearables, or athletic performance. LearnLaunch, a Boston-based accelerator, focuses on companies looking at using technology to transform education. There are others specific to augmented reality and virtual reality, blockchain, food, or defense. The kind of industry expertise that these programs can bring to bear on your startup is impressive.

The demo day at the end of an accelerator program is always a huge production with slick presentations that include walk-on music and a giant screen to project slides. The entrepreneur has five minutes to tell a story and give specifics about how their business works. There could be anywhere from 100 to 1,000 people in the audience to cheer on the startups. At the end, there is an ask, either for mentors or for investment. There's little opportunity to flex in the moment; everything is tightly scripted. And the pitch is mainly one way, with the entrepreneur giving their pitch without any Q&A.

This is a high-energy environment that feels like a combination of a graduation and a talent show. Each founder is putting on the best show they can as they demonstrate how far they have come during the accelerator experience. The audience is a friendly one, made up of investors, friends and family, community members, and other fans of entrepreneurship. Even though there is much support, this is a nerve-wracking proposition for a founder, since there's a lot on the line.

As is the case with every pitch opportunity, the founder should research which investors might be there, reach out via email to pitch why they would appreciate a meet-and-greet after the event, and then arrange to meet either at the networking reception that usually follows these presentations or at a later date.

OPEN PITCH COMPETITION

Opportunities to pitch abound. As you plug into your local or regional entrepreneurial community, you'll start to hear about various pitch competitions. They are usually industry-based.

In most instances, you will be required to fill out a written application to apply for consideration to pitch. If accepted, you can expect a kind of "show" environment, similar to the accelerator demo day, where you'll give a five to seven minute full-length pitch. Often there will be a good-sized audience present, full of people who are excited to hear about some of the newest local startups.

Get yourself geared up for a high energy show, thinking through how you can engage the audience and the judges from the get-go so that you stand out. Pitch competition implies a judging panel, so there will likely be a chunk of time for the Q&A section where the judges will ask questions after they've listened to your pitch.

Have fun with it! Any money won here is bonus money since it's equity free. The amounts vary by competition, usually five hundred to a few thousand dollars, but there are tons of benefits for standing out at an open pitch competition that go beyond money. It's great exposure in your local community, and who knows who will raise their hand with some help to offer as a result of your amazing pitch.

THE FAMILY OFFICE

Another audience to consider approaching for investment is a private funding source known as family offices. Family offices are private family foundations or funds that wealthy people establish to manage the family money. Family offices can be private groups that invest on behalf of one family, or a couple of families might band together and create a fund. While they are not often thought of as startup funding sources, family offices tend to have a wide portfolio of interests they invest in, so they invest in startups as a way to diversify their portfolio.

Unlike VCs, family offices aren't trying to get returns on, say, a ten-year fund. Rather, they are looking for generational wealth creation. Because of this and the fact that they are not beholden to LPs, their time horizon on an investment can be different. They may hold on to an investment longer without a liquidity event, and even reinvest further down the road if the startup continues to grow in a way that helps their main business or otherwise is favorable to them.

Also, family offices might back a startup for different reasons than your typical investor. They might be motivated to learn about a particular industry through investing in the startup or to grow a suitable partner for one of their other business lines. Finding a family office that can offer money and other resources relevant to your startup, such as industry connections or access to talent, can prove extremely beneficial to your company's future.

While two of the biggest family offices that invest in startups are owned by famous people—Pierre Omidyar, the founder of eBay, and Jeff Bezos, who started Amazon—the vast majority exist under the radar, valuing confidentiality and privacy above all else.

The bottom line with family offices? If you can find them and manage to engage them, mostly in small group meetings or one-on-one, they could prove willing to fund your startup. The tricky part is finding them, and that means research and networking. The people they hire to run their investing businesses tend to be experienced and sophisticated. Expect this process to remain formal throughout.

VENDORS AS FUNDING SOURCES

If your business falls into the consumer products category, as opposed to a tech company or a service provider, you might want to think about approaching vendors as investors. Often over-looked, vendors can be wonderful partners, not only because they could relieve your cash flow burden, but also because they are often more open than others to creative business arrangements. For example, you may be able to leverage vendor relationships to negotiate extended payment terms, or engage selected vendors directly to invest in your enterprise, especially vendors who might share your vision and get excited about becoming part of your company story.

These types of pitches tend to be more one-on-one and conversational with a big emphasis on the "what's in it for me" angle (for the vendor). Because you are only going to approach a vendor that you know well, you have the ability to adjust in real time as you sense how the pitch is received and where to go next. Sophistication varies, as vendors are not usually experienced investors, but most are good businesspeople, so they are looking to discuss this in business terms. Keep in mind that you are trying to pitch them the opportunity to join you in a big future, so it's important to put it into terms that relate to what they hope to achieve with their own company. You may recall in the story about Waku at the beginning of this chapter, Juan knew that his suppliers wanted to penetrate the U.S. market and was able to use this fact to convince them to become part of Waku's success.

RELATIONSHIPS WITH BANKERS

While bankers don't tend to invest in early-stage startups—they generally want two years of history for a business before they consider investing—it's never too early to develop a relationship with your banker, which is why I mention this here. Later, when you have that two-year history of growth, you will find all kinds of ways to leverage that good banking relationship.

As Terri Monjar, business banking VP at Bank of America, told me, "Think of developing your business credit history just like you think about building your personal credit history when you were younger. If you have a track record of paying bills on time and financial responsibility, it will help bankers feel much more comfortable lending you money."

Generally, community banks are more open to lending money to startups than big national or regional banks. However, the bigger banks might offer more products and services for your growing business. Keep this in mind when it's time to open your first business banking account for your startup; think about where you would be best off in the next phase of your company and the kinds of services a specific bank might offer to support you down the road.

Banks will want you to have collateral to secure a startup loan. This might mean putting up something in your personal portfolio of assets, such as your home or other investments. Understandably, going this route can be a bit terrifying for some entrepreneurs and should be thought through carefully.

When you feel like the time is right to pitch your banker, be sure you have a well-thought-out business plan to share, including detailed financial projections. If you have been building a relationship with your banker all along, they can be your champion in front of the lending committee and advocate within the bank to get you what you need.

GOVERNMENT-BACKED LOANS

Community Development Loan Funds (CDLFs) provide government-backed financing and development services to entrepreneurs who want to build businesses in low-income or economically distressed communities. Their mission is to expand economic opportunity and improve the quality of life for low-income people and communities. One way they do this is by helping people in these communities who might not ordinarily qualify for a bank loan get access to capital to start a company.

Micro-enterprises and small businesses, with ties to community development that will help spawn job growth and retention in hard-to-serve U.S. markets, can get loans from CDLFs certified by the Department of Treasury at a low interest rate. Like traditional bankers, this is a "high touch" model. Investors in these loan funds receive a modest, fixed rate of return, depending on current interest rates and the length of investment. During the period 2019-2020, these rates have ranged anywhere from 1.5 percent to 6 percent.

A local group oversees these loans. Local groups truly understand the context an entrepreneur is working in and will not only loan money but also offer assistance such as business training to help them succeed.

Going after one of these programs requires a superbly crafted pitch and a professional approach to a sophisticated investor. This can be an opportunity for an entrepreneur who doesn't have a traditional network to tap into for funding. The application process is similar to a bank loan process, but starts from the relationship an entrepreneur has with the local CDLF team, who are banking and finance professionals with a desire to invest in community development.

The US government's Small Business Administration also offers an online lender match program (a free referral tool at SBA.gov) to help you find SBA-approved lenders that could be right for your business based on various eligibility criteria.

NONPROFIT GRANTS

Grant-making institutions or foundations can be a good source of early-stage money. While it takes research to find a nonprofit that wants to invest in the kind of business you are building, having a social impact connected to your startup is good for business and makes this process easier.

You will still have to pitch your business, generally in a long-form written proposal, but this is in a sense "free money." You don't have to pay it back, and you don't have to give up equity in your business. You will, however, need to prove you spent it on what you said you would spend it on, and be able to show the impact.

Most foundations have a website that clearly explains their mission. Some are about empowering communities, some focus on education, others want to promote entrepreneurship. Learning what their mission is will help you customize your pitch to fit what they're trying to achieve. Foundations take into account many factors beyond just the pure financials of your startup, and most funding providers are experts in the cause they promote. Their definition of "ROI" can take on many meanings. Be sure to note any proposal due dates, as most operate on an annual schedule for giving out grant money.

STRATEGIC INVESTORS

Larger established companies often have built-in barriers to innovation, which causes them to seek strategic investment opportunities outside of their own corporate family. These companies look for opportunities to invest in or acquire a business on the cutting edge of their industry.

The upsides of seeking opportunities with strategic investors are numerous. Typically they are well funded and have loads of in-house expertise to help you realize your vision. Aligning yourself with them affords you credibility, and they can introduce you to potential customers and clients with whom they have strong relationships.

The downsides are that big companies are often risk-averse, meaning they might impose limitations on your activities, and they often move at a slower pace than you would like. Additionally, if you choose to align yourself with one giant in your industry, you will be cutting yourself off from everyone else.

Companies that might be viable strategic investors for you will become apparent as you develop your product and start to understand your target market. Keep your eyes on the competition; sometimes your biggest competitors end up being your best partners.

A bit of online investigation can go a long way to help you understand a company's strategy and direction. Once you've identified companies that align with your idea, the hardest part of approaching a potential strategic investor will be to reach the decision-makers.

While a warm introduction is usually best, sometimes these companies have pitch competitions, like Johnson & Johnson, VISA credit cards, and Anheuser-Busch InBev, to name a few. In fact, AB InBev feels so strongly about supporting innovative startups that they run their own new venture arm that incubates and invests in young companies. In 2019, they announced they had made over $1 billion in sales from these companies since they started in 2015.[26] Pharmacy chain CVS has also built their own digital innovation lab that seeks out startups, so keep an eye out for these types of arrangements as well.

The pitch for this kind of opportunity is usually quite formal with a committee of people from the company voting on the decision. Most have not worked in a startup, so understand that your context is unfamiliar to them. Be respectful of their process. While usually very strong businesspeople, they are not professional

---

26   Lucy Handley, "The world's largest brewer just made $1 billion from its new venture's arm – here's how," CNBC, July 24, 2019, https://www.cnbc.com/2019/07/24/ab-inbev-just-made-1-billion-from-innovation-group-zx-ventures.html.

investors, so they focus on what you can do to help their business, first and foremost.

CROWDFUNDING

Crowdfunding, the practice of funding a project or venture by raising small amounts of money from large numbers of people over the internet, has picked up steam over the last several years. For the early-stage entrepreneur, crowdfunding works well to get a venture off the ground, build buzz, and reach out to early adopters and influencers. It can also demonstrate to other investors that you are building something people really want.

Crowdfunding was made possible by the JOBS Act of 2012. JOBS is an acronym for "Jumpstart Our Business Startups." The law enables entrepreneurs to receive money in smaller increments from many people without fear of violating SEC regulations. In particular, the JOBS Act enables equity crowdfunding which allows people to own very small pieces of equity in startups. This is different from the donation-based type of crowdfunding like Kickstarter, Indiegogo, and GoFundMe.

With donation-based crowdfunding, you are giving something in return to people who invest in your startup. It may be a reward like an early look at the product, or you might offer people access to the product before anyone else can get it or at a lower price. Sometimes the reward is a T-shirt or some other token of appreciation.

To succeed with crowdfunding, you need to hone your marketing skills and know your target audience. Understanding how to leverage social media, email marketing, and organic and paid SEO are a plus to ensure your campaign stands out. All this means that you need to think hard about the target customer for your products so you can design the right way to drive awareness. For example, pre-launch selling to bolster a surge in support on the day you go live can amplify excitement and encourage social media shares. With crowdfunding, the name of the game is to generate buzz and garner as much interest as you can as early as possible. No one wants to jump into a crowdfunding opportunity that's a ghost town. Hence the "crowd" part. So you need to make it look like there's a groundswell of support right away for what you have to offer.

Most people investing in a crowdfunding campaign are not sophisticated investors. In fact, they'll see little, if any, financial information about the opportunity, so it's important that your pitch be compelling and reach out to them in a personal way. This is usually done with a two-minute video of you talking directly to the investor or contributor about your company. In the video, you explain your origin story, demo the product, and talk about your bigger vision, showcasing your own unique style. This video should look professional, and high quality sound and lighting are as important as is showcasing the product. Invite backers to join you on your startup journey and avoid making it sound transactional. You are going to want to send them updates to continue to engage them in new developments with your company. There's also room on your crowdfunding page for some long-form copy that you can use to pitch your startup.

It is perfectly acceptable to pound the pavement looking for several different types of investors at once. You never know where funding lightning will strike, so the more effort you put into your search, the likelier you are to reap results.

Of course, businesses don't run on funds alone. In the next chapter I'll introduce you to some sources for support beyond money.

CHAPTER 11

Pitching for More: Advisors, Influencers, Partners, and Press

UNRULY STUDIOS PARTNER STRATEGY

Bryanne Leeming was on a mission to help kids learn to code.

Her startup, Unruly Studios, had created their first product, Splats, to teach children coding through active play. Splats are light-up and sound-enhanced tiles that kids jump on as they learn to code new games on a connected app.

To further her mission, Bryanne needed to establish credibility in the education industry so she could build her company's reputation and find ways to garner support for acceleration.

Amon Millner, one of her key advisors and a thought leader in STEM, had helped her identify the Boston Children's Museum as a partner. The museum was known for innovation, as well as for supporting new research that offered insights on the power of play for children's developing brains.

Leveraging Amon's network, Bryanne received several introductions to influential people at the museum. She started slow, getting to know key museum people and figuring out how to fit Unruly Studios into the institution's overall strategic agenda.

Eventually, through deliberate networking, Unruly Studios was accepted to participate as an exhibitor at the Boston Children Museum's Maker Faire where she could demo the Splats for the community of educators, parents, and young kids who frequented museum events.

Not only did she learn feedback on Splats, but also she was able to meet several members of the museum's leadership attending the event, who showed a keen interest in learning more about her company's mission.

Armed with intelligence about the museum's experimental bent and its particular interest in finding new ways to engage kids, as gleaned from her strategic networking, Bryanne was able to arrange a formal meeting with museum leaders. Leveraging this intelligence in her pitch, Bryanne delivered a spot-on presentation. Museum leaders offered Unruly Studios and Splats a place in their Tech Kitchen pilot program, a venue for Boston tech innovators to showcase new products and encourage museum-goers to try them.

The day the program launched, there was a line of kids out the door of the museum waiting to try Splats for themselves. Not only was Splats a huge hit with adult museum-goers and their kids, but also the feedback was priceless for development. The museum had been a perfect platform for the new product and created an army of early adopters, excited and clamoring to help. The museum was almost as thrilled as Bryanne, having received proof that this new exhibit format would attract the new generation of museum visitors they wanted to reach.

As the relationship grew, Bryanne received more opportunities to associate with the museum. She was learning from them, and they were engaging new audiences through her. At the second Maker Faire, she met a Somerville, Massachusetts, public school teacher who decided to pilot Splats throughout the city's school system.

Bryanne's initial partnership with the Boston Children's Museum had given her the credibility she needed to attract the school system, meet key advisors, and apply for grant money to fuel the growth of Unruly Studios.

Entrepreneur Bryanne Leeming understood one of the most important success factors in launching a new venture: startups don't succeed by money alone.

Along with fundraising, she knew finding the right mentors and advisors, attending the right networking events, jumping on opportunities to showcase her invention, and pitching for connections, were what she needed. These activities achieved recognition among people who could help get her startup off the ground.

This book is subtitled *Winning Money, Mentors, and More for Your Startup* for a reason. Sometimes, as Bryanne knew well, success or failure can hinge on how much effort you put into the *More*.

When people think of investors, they automatically default to funders. But there are different types of investors whose affiliation with your enterprise can be worth more than money at the end of the day. I am talking about advisory board members, early adopters, industry influencers, and the media.

ADVISORY BOARDS

People are judged by the company they keep, and so are startups. One of the best ways you can enhance your company's reputation and bolster your ability to get your business in front of the right people is to bring on a board of advisors.

Establishing an advisory board early on helps you connect with influential businesspeople who can guide you on your startup journey. Try to attract advisory board members who can serve as mentors and who have a network of like-minded industry leaders.

It is important to be very clear on what you ask these people to do. Are your expectations that they will be available to meet you on a regular basis? Do you want to attend their networking events? Access to their contacts? What will be their role, if any, in decision-making? Set all expectations at the outset, and you'll avoid issues that could develop later.

Keep in mind that when you ask someone to be on your advisory board, you are asking for their time and connections, and this is significant. It is up to you to convince them that you are worth this kind of investment. Be prepared to pitch them one-on-one like you would a monetary investment prospect. Do the same amount of research and afford them the same degree of courtesy as you would any other potential investor.

You will probably want to offer advisory board members at least a small amount of equity in your company as compensation. Not only does this demonstrate to them that you value their professional input and hold them in high esteem, but it also gives them a real stake in the business, hopefully an added incentive to see your company succeed.

Your advisory board does not need to be big. It is typical at first to have only two or three people. But keep in mind that members will likely change over time as your business evolves. It's not unusual for the type and configuration of a company's advisory board to change, much like the company itself changes and grows. For example, some startups, as they expand into new markets, will create a customer advisory board to help them create business development plans to reach new consumers.

EARLY ADOPTERS

Take advantage of opportunities to connect with early adopters of your product, technology, or services. As soon as you have any kind of product launched, even if it's only your MVP, spend time with those first users and understand their experience using it.

There is no better way to get genuine insights into your products than to reach out to the first people who put their money down to buy what you are offering.

You can learn a ton about how your product needs to evolve, or whether you have the wrong customer in mind. Maybe you were targeting college students when in reality it's the yoga mom who ended up loving your product first.

It's useful to court your early adopters. Your pitch to these people is about giving them a first look at improvements or new releases. You want to give them a heads-up about big news with your company before it's announced to the world. It's not a formal pitch per se, but it's more that you are sharing with them your vision for the world and asking them to join the journey with you by being an early customer.

Proceeding this way also helps manage their expectations if things don't work exactly as promised (as is often the case at this stage). They can be more forgiving when they know the back story of the product and what you are trying to achieve. Bring them inside to see what's behind the curtain of your startup.

They may even have a big social presence, and if they become passionate about your company and start talking about it on their social channels, that's another marketing channel you can leverage toward your growth. You can help them share information about your company by providing them with discount codes they can give out, such as invitations to the "closed" beta launch they can offer their colleagues, or giving them some kind of bonus for helping you attract new customers in your earliest stage.

INDUSTRY INFLUENCERS

Another group to pitch is industry influencers. Early adopters are generally people who found your product organically in the course of following their passions. Influencers develop a community of followers who see them as a thought leader. They are careful to maintain a certain standard of communication with their markets to align with their personal brand.

Every community of interest in the world has influencers. For instance, in the online gaming world you'll find different influencers for each well-known game on the market. These people are recognized as leaders in a certain game community. They are experts, relied upon to stay ahead of trends. They know things that others don't know, such as whether and when a new version will be released.

Generally, influencers want some kind of compensation for promoting a product, but it's not always money. You could, for example, offer them a free item to demo. There is an obvious difference in motivation and expectation for an influencer. They might not expect remuneration directly from you, but they do expect it in the number of social media hits and likes, or exposure that being involved with your product brings to them.

Regardless of industry, the point of connecting with influencers is for them to create buzz about what you're doing. They will only create buzz if they genuinely believe in your product and are excited about it; otherwise, it hurts their credibility. Others trust them, which is why they're so powerful in spreading ideas and trends.

Some entrepreneurs hope to get a celebrity to endorse their product, but the odds of this are very small; plus, it can cost a lot of money. Sometimes choosing to stay focused is a better play. Finding a micro-influencer or industry influencer who has captured the bullseye of your target market can be a better use of time and money.

The pitch for influencers must take into account their motivations and goals. You should tailor your pitch to make sure it includes a specific rationale for them to get involved with you, how it will help them to meet their own goals as a thought leader.

PITCHING FOR PR

Public Relations, or PR, is hands down the most effective and cost-efficient way to drive awareness and win attention once your company is launched. The beauty of PR, or earned media as it is sometimes called, is that you don't have to pay for it. Instead, you get the media to pay attention to you because you have a great story and you know how to tell it.

Good PR is all about timing. You don't want your PR to create expectations you can't meet. For instance, you wouldn't want to do a great job promoting a product that isn't ready for market, only to end up with a large number of orders and no capacity for fulfillment.

Don't approach the press about your business until you're ready, but when you are, go for it with gusto.

The process of getting a journalist to write about you is similar to the process of finding an investor or a mentor. You start by doing your research. Whether it's SaaS technology, nutrition beverages, consumer finance, or sustainable fashion, there are journalists devoted to writing about specific things. When you approach them to make your pitch for an interview, demonstrate that you know what they care about. Make the connection for them so they know you're not wasting their time. They are true professionals and want to be appreciated for their craft. Show them you singled them out for a reason.

And, please please, do not send out boring old press releases to journalists. A press release is not a good way to approach media people. They don't read them and don't care about them. You need to approach media people so that they will tell your story the way you want them to, but it also needs to work for them.

Journalists say that if you have an interesting story, you should email them. But an email needs to be very specific about why you think you have something they will want to write about. When you pitch them to write about you, be very clear about why your story is special. Show yourself as a good spokesperson for your company; be open and interesting. This might mean offering to provide some inside scoop about a product release or other big news. Remember what's important to you may not be important to them. You need to find that common ground and present it in a pitch that is clear and brief.

Another way to develop relationships with journalists is to offer your help. Without demanding anything in return, such as recognition in the piece, offer facts or a point of view that you know could be useful to them in their writing. When you give a journalist a solid line, they are going to remember you the next time they need a source for a story. Once you have established rapport, they will be more than happy to write about you when the time and the story are right.

You might also consider joining a service called HARO (help a reporter out) at the website helpareporter.com, where you can sign up to become a source for journalists writing stories in your wheelhouse. You'll get daily emails inviting you to pitch to become a quoted expert for a journalist's story. This will get your name and the name of your company associated with your industry and in front of people who follow industry news.

Building relationships to further your business interests takes a great deal of time and effort, both during your startup phases and throughout the life of your business. In fact, as all seasoned entrepreneurs will tell you, you will never stop pitching for investment, for sales, and to build the relationships you need to be successful.

Final Thoughts

PITCHING NEVER ENDS

Entrepreneurship is one of the most powerful forces for change in the world. Startups solve all kinds of problems, from how to recycle plastics piling up in landfills, to how to get temporary wheels when you're a carless college kid, to how to teach young children to code so they can be ready when it's time to invent the next generation of technology to improve our lives.

Entrepreneurship is a team sport, and to succeed in any new venture, you need help from funders, mentors, advisors, customers, and more.

PITCH OR PERISH

Communicating the what, the why, and the how of your startup in a memorable and compelling way is vital to getting the people you need—investors, mentors, and more—on board with what you're doing.

Your pitch tells the story of your business. And that story, whether relayed in your value proposition statement, your email to a new connection, your elevator pitch, your presentation deck, or your leave-behind deck, should represent the venture in a consistent and concise fashion with all the pieces aligned.

Be sure you make time to practice. And then practice some more. You can never practice enough. As you get better at your pitch, you'll feel more confident on your feet and able to handle whatever happens in the moment. Being quick on your feet is not only an extremely good feeling, it is also a skill you'll use in many situations.

As you address different audiences, you will receive feedback. Every meeting you take, every presentation you make, every time you practice your pitch in front of colleagues, family, and friends, you'll learn something new about how well your message is getting across, about whether and to what extent people understand what you're saying and want to learn more. Each time you pitch, you will be in front of someone who brings their own perspectives and experiences. Pitching becomes a way to pressure-test questions you may have about your model and people's reaction to it. You are not giving your pitch in a vacuum, and it's not ultimately about you. Remember, you are taking your audience on a journey.

In the early days of your startup, you'll make decisions that will affect the trajectory of your company. Having a strong value proposition that you believe you can deliver becomes a filter for all these decisions. Your pitch expands on your priorities and culture, and therefore your company's direction. As your company evolves, so will your pitch. And perhaps surprisingly, the reverse is also true.

As you continue to work with and develop your pitch, you'll find the process instrumental in helping you move your business forward. There is a heightening of thought that shines through every time you work on your pitch—a particular turn of phrase, a change of emphasis on a point that you now realize has altered in its importance to your value proposition—that produces epiphanies. Expect to experience "aha" moments, as a pivot in phrasing propels evolution in thought.

PITCHING IS PERSONAL

Never sit across from a potential investor, mentor, or advisor you haven't researched thoroughly. Never.

I've said it before, but it bears repeating (and repeating): *pitching is personal.*

You want to know as much as possible about the person you are going to be sitting down with or about the people in the audience of your presentation. Think about ways to make a real connection with them as you pitch, during the question and answer session, or in your follow-up.

What you want to do is create a strong emotional connection so the person you are pitching can't help but want to join you on this journey.

NETWORK, NETWORK, NETWORK

Network like crazy. Join everything. Go everywhere. See and be seen. In most cities and metro regions, there are events every week for startups and entrepreneurs to learn together or just socialize. Things like open pitch competitions, industry panels, and "how to" workshops for entrepreneurs are places to find like-minded people. Find where your local startup community hangs out and grab a seat. Be open to conversation and think about how you can be helpful to others. That's actually one of the best places to start.

Have coffee with as many people as you can. Make the invitation. Buy the cup of Joe. Don't stand on ceremony. If you want a seat at the pitch table, it's going to take hustle. And coffee. Lots and lots of coffee.

A note about how you approach this: if you are inviting a busy person to coffee, have a specific ask. I can't even count the number of requests I receive from people who want to buy me a cup of coffee so they can "pick my brain." Not only does that sound painful, it isn't being respectful of my time. I'll let you in on a secret. For most busy people, that kind of generic request is going to get you the opposite reaction of what you are hoping for. Make it easy for people to give you advice by zeroing in on exactly what kind of help you are looking for at that time. Help them help you.

You've done all the work of creating connections; now is your chance to have a key person's attention for twenty minutes, which will hopefully turn into fifty minutes. If they like what they hear, they will ask specific questions and maybe push back on some of your assumptions to see how you respond. Ideally they will be interested and want to go to the next level.

And finally, be nice. Always. You never know who is around. Believe in kismet. Strange (and wonderful) things happen.

One of my students was in line at a café wearing a Babson sweatshirt. The guy standing behind her in line had gone to Babson and he happened to be a family office investment manager for a large group of families. They started a conversation with him simply asking her what she was working on. She launched into her amazing elevator pitch, and he was intrigued by the digital health business she was building. He asked more questions and more questions, and she was delighted to give him all the answers. This chance encounter and resulting conversation led to a meeting. Then, he invited her to pitch to the family office. You know what happened next. They invested.

THIS IS NOT THE END

Your plans for your company's future might include bringing in partners, acquiring another enterprise, undergoing a merger, or being acquired. Whether you move toward your goals slowly, or you experience exponential growth in one quantum leap, you will need to secure resources to help you get to the next level.

Conquering milestones doesn't happen solo. Success with startups takes a village.

And so, you will pitch.

Resources for Developing Your Pitch

Below are some helpful resources and tools for your pitch, many of which I mention in this book. Because these types of resources are constantly being updated, I offer a more extensive list at my website, thefirstpitchbook.com.

RESOURCES FOR DESIGNING PITCH DECKS

- The Noun Project: a huge array of icons to use in a pitch deck
- Startupstockphotos.com: a resource for stock images and pictures for your deck
- Unsplash: high quality images that are not copy-protected
- Canva: free (and paid) templates to design your own marketing materials
- Slidebean: examples of pitch decks and templates to design your own deck

- Piktochart: offers great templates for decks, infographics, and other marketing materials for DIY (free and paid versions)
- Sketchbubble: templates and icons to create presentation decks
- 99designs, Fiverr, and Upwork: online marketplaces to find freelance designers for all kinds of pitch communication including deck design and logos
- SketchDeck: find designers you can hire for pitch deck creation, presentations, and logo development

EXAMPLES OF GOOD PITCH DECKS CAN BE FOUND HERE:

- Cirrus Insight Startup Pitch Decks: https://www.cirrusinsight.com/blog/startup-pitch-decks
- 30 Legendary Startup Pitch Decks And What You Can Learn From Them: https://piktochart.com/blog/startup-pitch-decks-what-you-can-learn/
- LinkedIn SlideShare: slideshare.net (search pitch decks)

RESOURCES TO LEARN ABOUT INVESTORS:

- Angel Capital Association (angelcapitalassociation.org): directory of active angels and angel groups in the United States
- National Venture Capital Association (nvca.org): information about the venture capital industry, has some resources and an online listing of their members
- Crunchbase: offers a newsletter that provides information about startups and fundraising; also has investment listings for all public and private companies so you can see who funded them and when

- Pitchbook: provides data about VC, PE, and M&A transactions, including public and private companies, investors, funds, firms, and people
- AngelList: a platform for startups to raise money online, recruit employees, and apply for funding; also has a good blog

OTHER HELPFUL TOOLS:

- Hubspot, Insightly, Salesforce, Pipedrive, Mailchimp, Conspire: all offer CRM solutions and email tracking software for small- and medium-sized businesses
- DocSend provides a system to track and send large documents via email easily
- HARO (Help a reporter out) is a resource to find press opportunities to contribute your expertise and meet journalists in your industry
- Balsamiq is a resource to create software mockups and wireframes to facilitate discussion and understanding before any code is written

CROWDFUNDING RESOURCES:

- Crowdfunding sites: Indiegogo, Kickstarter
- Equity crowdfunding: SeedInvest, Republic, Wefunder, StartEngine

RESOURCES FOR ENTREPRENEURS (GENERAL):

- TechStars Toolkit: https://toolkit.techstars.com/
- Kauffman Foundation FASTTRAC toolkit: https://www.fasttrac.org/green/

Acknowledgments

Thank you to all the amazing student and alumni entrepreneurs at Babson. You've taught me so much. You inspire me with your drive and creativity. My job doesn't feel like a job because of you.

I am especially grateful to the entrepreneurs who shared the details of their stories for this book: Bryanne Leeming, Michael and Matthew Vega-Sanz, David Zamarin, Juan Giraldo and Nicolas Estrella, Dan Schorr, Jeff Avallon, Mayuresh Soni and Kazunori Kawanobe, Ravish Majithia, Ashley and Jerry Taylor, Jamie Steenbakkers and Michael Leahy, and Emily Levy.

And to the amazing Babson faculty—Candida Brush, Andrew Corbett, Mark Rice, Phillip Kim, Sharon Sinnott, Susan Duffy, Bill Gartner, Heidi Neck, Angelo Santinelli, Beth Goldstein, Lakshmi Balachandra, Erik Noyes, and Les Charm—whose knowledge and teaching informed much of this book and whom I greatly admire. I feel honored to work with you and call you my colleagues.

Thanks to the Blank Center team—Antonette Ho, Cindy Klein-

Marmer, Alexandra Dunk, Nancy McCarthy, Tamara Lamenzo, and Beth Peterson—for being awesome and never letting any balls drop, even when we seem to keep adding more.

A huge thanks to my friends Michael Dearing, Diane Hessan, Andrew Klopfer, David Chang, Jeff Bussgang, Sarah Hodges, Jamie Goldstein, and John Landry for providing investor perspective; and Ilyse Greenberg, Brent Turner, and Josh Bernoff for sharing your creative and smart ideas for the book.

I am so grateful for my incredible family—Brent, my best friend and collaborator; Seth and Cole, who I could not be more proud of; and, of course, Max the most amazing dog, who sat with me every day as I wrote this book. Thanks for keeping me focused on getting this book done, loving me when I'm crazy, and making me laugh when I'm down. Thanks and love to my parents and sisters who are my best cheerleaders.

Massive appreciation for Nancy Wollin, my writing buddy. It was so fun and energizing to work with you. And thanks to editor extraordinaire Martha Lanning, hunter of the passive voice.

Gratitude for the multi-talented Ralph Haddad for making a beautiful website to support the book at thefirstpitchbook.com.

And finally, I want to thank all the great educators, entrepreneurs, and investors who, by generously sharing their knowledge and experiences, make it easier for everyone working with and in startups to be more successful. You are helping to change the world!

About the Author

DEBI KLEIMAN is the executive director of the Arthur M. Blank Center for Entrepreneurship at Babson College, where she works with students, alumni, staff, and faculty, as well as the broader entrepreneurial community, to accelerate the practice of entrepreneurship. She leads the Blank Center's strategy, new initiatives, and team to help develop the programs of the Butler Launch Pad and Babson's highly-rated entrepreneur experiences, such as the B.E.T.A. Challenge New Venture Competition, Rocket Pitch, and the Summer Venture Program.

Debi has oversight for Babson's major entrepreneurship academic research platforms: the BCERC Conference and the Global Entrepreneurship Monitor (GEM) U.S. Report. She is also an adjunct professor at Babson's F.W. Olin Graduate School of Business and Executive Education Programs for Entrepreneurs.

Before coming to Babson, Debi was the managing director and executive vice president at Havas Media in Boston. Prior to that, she was president of the Massachusetts Innovation and Technology Exchange (MITX), and she served as an executive at C-space (formerly Communispace) for five years before its sale to Omnicom DAS. Earlier in her career, she led marketing for two early-stage tech startups as part of their founding teams.

Debi has been an advisor to startups, served on many boards, and been an advocate for Boston's innovation community for over fifteen years. She has mentored entrepreneurs at top tier accelerators such as MassChallenge, Harvard's iLab and Tech-Stars. Before finding her passion for startups, she held marketing leadership roles at Procter & Gamble, Welch's, and the Coca-Cola Company.

Debi has a BS from Cornell University and an MBA from Harvard Business School.

She lives outside of Boston with her husband, two teenage sons and big furry rescue dog.

Made in the USA
Middletown, DE
23 June 2023

32967192R00137